With disarming vulne[...]
willing to own their w[...]
God who heals. The pathway? A "surrender in our bodily life [that] leads to surrender in our spiritual life." Fabian gently encourages us to draw near to God by "engag[ing] with the world physically" through reframed classical practices like embodied prayer and sharing a meal. But she also winsomely introduces the reader to fresh, inviting avenues of healing, like laughter (our "protest against suffering") and "digging in the dirt," which helps us humbly "ground ourselves" in the sovereign arms of the God who created it. There's no shame and guilt here; only a grace-filled invitation to the arms of a Father who loves us freely and forever.

J. KEVIN BUTCHER, executive director of Rooted Ministries, author of *Choose and Choose Again* and *Free*

Whenever Kellye Fabian has something to say, I listen. Her wisdom and pastoral guidance shine brightly in *Holy Vulnerability*. Immerse yourself in these beautiful words and practices, and let the Holy Spirit teach you how to be both fully human and deeply loved.

CATHERINE McNIEL, author of *Long Days of Small Things* and *All Shall Be Well*

HOLY VULNERABILITY

spiritual practices
for the broken,

ashamed,

anxious &

afraid

holy
vulnerability

KELLYE FABIAN

A NavPress resource published in alliance
with Tyndale House Publishers

NavPress is the publishing ministry of The Navigators, an international Christian organization and leader in personal spiritual development. NavPress is committed to helping people grow spiritually and enjoy lives of meaning and hope through personal and group resources that are biblically rooted, culturally relevant, and highly practical.

For more information, visit NavPress.com.

Holy Vulnerability: Spiritual Practices for the Broken, Ashamed, Anxious, and Afraid

Copyright © 2021 by Kellye Fabian. All rights reserved.

A NavPress resource published in alliance with Tyndale House Publishers

NAVPRESS and the NavPress logo are registered trademarks of NavPress, The Navigators, Colorado Springs, CO. *TYNDALE* is a registered trademark of Tyndale House Ministries. Absence of ® in connection with marks of NavPress or other parties does not indicate an absence of registration of those marks.

The Team:
Caitlyn Carlson, Acquisitions Editor; Elizabeth Schroll, Copy Editor; Olivia Eldredge, Operations Manager; Julie Chen, Designer

Cover photograph of hands by Nathan Dumlao on Unsplash. All rights reserved.

Author photo by New Branch Films, copyright © 2016. All rights reserved.

Author is represented by The Christopher Ferebee Agency, www.christopherferebee.com.

For information about special discounts for bulk purchases, please contact Tyndale House Publishers at csresponse@tyndale.com, or call 1-855-277-9400.

ISBN 978-1-63146-932-9

Printed in the United States of America

27	26	25	24	23	22	21
7	6	5	4	3	2	1

For the broken, ashamed, anxious, and afraid . . .

for all of us.

Contents

Foreword

*O*ne time, Kellye invited me to speak to her small-group leaders. Kris and I sat comfortably at one of the tables as Kellye spoke to her leaders. While sitting, I had what many at Willow Creek Community Church call a "prompting." These are not common experiences for me, so I knew I had one. I told Kellye that evening that she should go to (our!) seminary, so Kellye and I met not long after at a favorite coffee shop, and we talked. I should say Kellye—ever the lawyer—asked me questions, good questions, questions not normally asked by future seminary students. Her questions were about what goes on in classes and why she should take classes and what she would learn. I don't remember details, but what I have said to many is this: "You will like seminary not for what it will do *for* you but what it will do *to* you."

The book you are holding in your hands, *Holy Vulnerability*, reveals in part what the Lord has done *to* Kellye in the last four years as she has pondered the Bible and theology. I cannot tell you what an honor it was for me when she asked me to write the foreword. In reading this book, I see through her clear-as-glass prose to her vulnerable heart before God and now vulnerable before all of us. Kellye sat in classes with alert eyes, taking notes but pondering (in her inimitable manner) what was said. She was a quiet student, but when Kellye spoke, students listened. She spoke out of an authentic life, out of a deep pondering of the Lord at work in her life, out of a clear mind with compelling arguments, and out of a holy concern for the church where she found faith and where she is nurturing the faith of others. Willow Creek has a gift from God in Kellye.

Kellye's authentic vulnerability percolates in this book in a disarming manner. She speaks from her own brokenness, which she has at times confessed to me. She speaks about shame and about anxiety and about fear. Because she's been through so much, she speaks almost fearlessly and unselfconsciously about her own struggles. She doesn't thunder with prophetic words about how wrong these are, nor does she offer any simplistic solutions. No, she disarms us by explaining how she lives with these kinds of experiences as she prays and walks with the Lord and communes with her husband and with friends. Many will find in Kellye, simply by reading this book, a mother-confessor because she gently leads others to see their own reality. Our class flew to Istanbul and visited, with a couple more flights, biblical sites in Turkey, Greece, and Italy. Kellye explained to me with a disarming honesty her dread and fear of flying. She didn't back away from it, she just moved forward into yet another experience of trusting God in the midst of anxiety and fear. Her persona is put together, but she knows what's in her heart and she will tell you—honestly, vulnerably.

While this book is personal, it is not at all self-absorbed. One of the gifts of good writers of familiar essays is that they tell their own stories in a way that tells our own story too. This book does this on every page: Her story is the story of others. Time and time again as I read *Holy Vulnerability*, I thought of the Psalms, by far the most vulnerable and personal book in the Bible. In the Psalms, there are more than fifteen hundred uses of first-person pronouns: I, my, and me. That's not counting first person plurals: We, our, and us. The Psalms map for us a path into a personal experience of God as well as our personal experiences with God. Our experiences with God are often discovered in the presence of others, a major focus of Kellye's book. Spiritual formation that is entirely individualistic fails the basic test of the Bible: The *I* of the Psalms and the entire Bible is an I that is one part of a *We*.

One of the highlights of *Holy Vulnerability* comes to expression in the many, varied writers she quotes. I know some of them were from readings in her classes. They show that she didn't read them for the assignment or the paper but to suck the marrow from each writer for how they could feed her faith. Reflective students take in more than the rest.

Scot McKnight

Introduction

O God, you are my God;
I earnestly search for you.
My soul thirsts for you;
my whole body longs for you
in this parched and weary land
where there is no water.

PSALM 63:1

$\mathscr{T}$he words of this first verse of Psalm 63 expose a deep longing within me. I feel it in my body—a sense that something is missing . . . but also that the desire can be met. Much of the time, I struggle to know what to do with this thirst. It's like the psalmist describes—I'm searching, hands grasping and eyes darting in desperation.

Jesus gave us the answer. He said, "Let anyone who is thirsty come to me and drink" (John 7:37, NIV). But how? How do we come to him? How do we allow him to satisfy our thirst?

For centuries, spiritual practices have been an intentional way Christians have quieted their hearts and sought to draw near to Jesus. Let's be honest, though—spiritual practices can sound like an invitation to the elite, those who have "made it" spiritually. They have hours to reflect and pray. They burn candles and have easier access to God's presence. They think only of God and never watch silly television shows or read novels. There's nothing wrong with any of these super-spiritual-seeming things, but they can seem a bit unrealistic to most of us. After all, we have demanding jobs, aging parents, rambunctious toddlers, ministries in need of our time, relationships to build and sustain.

Now, don't get me wrong—I long to be spiritually mature. I love candles, and yes, I struggle with the ultimate meaning of seemingly mundane tasks and entertainment. I can find myself envying the image I have of the people who seem to have it all together spiritually. But when I return to the Gospels, I am struck again and again by the truth that Jesus (while inviting all) didn't really come for the spiritually elite. Instead, he took great care to seek out the broken in body and mind. He looked for those who had no honor, the ones who were shamed because of their social position or physical condition. He met at night with the afraid. He had eyes to see and words to share with the anxiety-ridden. Jesus even said, "Healthy people don't need a doctor—sick people do. . . . I have come to call not those who think they are righteous, but those who know they are sinners" (Matthew 9:12-13). So, I guess without putting too fine of a point on it, he came for me and you. In fact, have you ever noticed how the spiritual elite of Jesus' day didn't really like him, primarily because he hung around people like us? You know, the broken, ashamed, anxious, and afraid.

And . . . I've got to be honest—I'm all of those things.

I am a chronic worrier. The experts call it "generalized anxiety," which means I am anxious about everyday things most of the time without any discernible reason. You wouldn't necessarily know this about me because I come across as calm even when things around me are in chaos. But my insides are usually roiling with worry. Often I couldn't tell you what is causing my anxiousness. I haven't been able to sort out the original source of my worried soul, but in some ways, my anxiety has become like that friend you can't quite cut ties with. Even though you don't enjoy their company, they've just been around for too long to do anything drastic at this point. I've been aware of this anxiety issue for years, but I have always thought it was associated with particular experiences or situations. It turns out, though, that worry is a pretty constant state for me. In fact, I've become so used to this friend that I thought what I was experiencing was just a normal part of being human. Turns out, this isn't totally true.

Along with my anxiety, I also suffer from a healthy dose of fear. Anxiety about flying transforms easily into fear during the flight. Fear can come along all by itself, too— like when I'm running on the treadmill in a hotel gym by myself, and before a minute passes, I'm thinking of the guy who died in a hotel gym by himself while running on a treadmill, leaving his wife and kids behind in a pile of grief. *I probably shouldn't be here running alone.* Then a different kind of fear springs up a few minutes later when a man walks by the glass doorway of the gym. I'm a woman in a closed space with no one around—my whole body jumps. Adrenaline pours into my bloodstream, my heart races, and sweat slicks over my hands. Several minutes pass before I am convinced I am safe. As with my anxiety, I can't quite trace the origin of the fear I experience. I figure there is a lot to be afraid of in our world. Bad things do happen to women running alone, and people have died running on treadmills. It's not like my fears are unfounded.

And then there's shame. Shame is sneaky and pernicious because it gets me questioning my own worth and worthiness. I have shame around body image, and just my image generally—not being able to respond quickly in an argument or debate, being un-"liked," making mistakes, and perhaps most insulting and ironic, struggling with anxiety and fear. I've had a hard time recognizing where I experience shame because, of all things, I didn't want to admit that I experience it at all. As a friend recently shared an encounter with shame, I listened and empathized—then told her that my struggles aren't really with shame, but in other areas. She is wise enough to know this wasn't true but gracious enough not to point that out in the moment. I have shame about feeling shame.

Also, something in me—something that is pretty fundamental—is broken. I certainly learned early on in life about sin (I went to a Catholic grade school and high school, after all). But when was it that I realized that despite my best efforts—best intended, best executed—sometimes I simply couldn't help but make hurtful decisions? I have made and continue to make so many choices that arise out of this brokenness I carry around. And this doesn't even include the harmful things I say and do without intention. When did I break? How can I be mended and made whole?

I suspect I'm not alone in living in this tangled mess. There's something profoundly human in all of this, a universal experience of holding ourselves together in the midst of falling apart. And if it's true that Jesus came for the likes of you and me, how exactly does he seek to heal all this anxiety and fear and shame and brokenness? What did he come to do, and how do we get in on whatever that is? I know for some this question must seem super basic—the kind of thing you'd learn around age five in Sunday school. Jesus died for our sins, and when we believe in him, we have eternal life. Yes, yes, yes. And—there is so much more. Believing certain things about Jesus is, of course, part of it; and generally we're pretty good at working on and expressing what we believe. But, again, when I look at the Gospels, what I see first is an invitation to walk with, to watch, *to participate*. We don't save ourselves—but once we are saved in the most fundamental of ways, Jesus invites us to join him in the larger healing of our brokenness.

These invitations from Jesus, in fact, are far more common than the invitation to believe. Those who sought out Jesus did so not for eternal salvation, or even forgiveness, but for some kind of physical or mental healing. In our day, we seem to think we're supposed to do the opposite. First, we are to believe certain things about Jesus, and then we look to him to answer our requests for healing. We've been taught that Jesus cares more about our spiritual state than our physical well-being. This may seem true given the way we emphasize the state of our hearts and souls as a barometer of faith, but perhaps by focusing only on the spiritual side of things, we have missed something crucial in how Jesus heals. Perhaps the only window we have into our true spiritual state—our rebellion against God and his ways—is our physical and mental brokenness, our shame, anxiety, and fear. If we listened to our addictions, shame spirals, panic attacks, and disabling fears instead of trying to flee from them . . . those very things could lead us to a healing encounter with God. In other words, recognizing our physical and mental ailments in God's presence leads to a spiritual turning around (repentance) and healing. This participation is Jesus' primary invitation, the most intimate and revolutionary way we get to encounter him in our lives.

When I first cried out to Jesus, I wasn't looking for eternal salvation. I wasn't looking for forgiveness. I needed help in my temporal, physical life. Something was wrong. I was doing things I didn't want to do, but I felt helpless to turn things around. I was desperate and would do almost anything to find a way out. We see this pattern in Scripture, too. Luke tells the story of a paralyzed man who was so desperate to be physically healed so he could walk again (and be welcomed into community instead of shunned because of his condition) that he had his friends carry him on his mat onto the roof of the building where Jesus was teaching. They devised some kind of pulley system, dug a hole through the roof tiles, and lowered him into Jesus' presence (Luke 5:17-19). There is no indication in the text that the man or his friends desired anything other than physical healing. Here they were before God incarnate, and their minds and hearts were focused on the temporal—the man's broken body. What he needed was healing. And it was worth going through the humiliation he must have felt being lowered through a roof in front of a gaping crowd to get it. He would do anything.

A woman who had a disorder that caused constant bleeding for a dozen years had a similar compulsion to bring her broken body near to Jesus (Luke 8:43-48). We can imagine that as she trained her eyes on Jesus with the hope of getting close enough to touch his robe, she was thinking about finally being cured of the thus-far incurable. There is no indication that she was seeking eternal help. She needed help with her broken body. And she would endure venturing out before the public, those who believed she was unclean, shameful, and even cursed, to be healed. She would do anything.

While we read many stories of physical healing in the

Gospels, people with internal brokenness, invisible shame, disabling fear, and disquieting anxiety also sought out Jesus. Zacchaeus, a tax collector, felt trapped by his own greed and desire for power. Something in him continued to allow him to rip off his own people to get rich. Indeed, the people in his neighborhood referred to him as a "notorious sinner" (Luke 19:7). When we read of his repentance, he seems to be longing to get out from under the shame associated with his actions and make those he had cheated more than whole again.

In each of these encounters with Jesus, the person involved sought Jesus out. In none did Jesus barge in unwanted or uninvited. He did offer more than each was seeking, it seems—eternal healing as well as temporal. But they had to present themselves before him and acknowledge their need for help. They didn't come quietly—theirs were desperate cries, demanding calls, longing prayers.

What I have discovered in the last few years (and of course this is no real revelation to those who have walked this road before me) is that God longs to be invited into my brokenness, anxiety, fear, and shame. It is in these very sensitive, hurting, and sometimes bleeding wounds that I experience God's real presence and my thirst is relieved. Not to mention, God transforms us in these places and begins to mend what's broken and heal what hurts. I can only be helped in his presence.

These wounds hurt, though, and I have become practiced at protecting them from perceived harm. I have developed many ways of coping to avoid dealing with and facing these wounds. I have built strong walls, and they withstand even the most sincere and gentle attempts to get in. For the most part, my resistance has been unintentional and reflexive. These areas are so sensitive. I don't want anyone seeing them, moving around in them, or trying to change anything. It will hurt!

But—the presence of Jesus awaits me on the other side of the wall. Healing and freedom are only possible on the other side of the wall. If I am to meet Jesus there, I must begin to dismantle all of the ways I keep him out and open myself to ways to let him in.

Something lingers in the back of my mind, and I suspect it might linger in all of our minds. Jesus is not physically here. When we live in the first half of the twenty-first century and desperately want to follow his plea to come to him, or to go to him for healing as those alive in the first century did, what do we do? We can't make an appointment with him on our day off. We won't run into him at the grocery store after work.

This is where spiritual practices come in. They open us, help us lower the walls, and bring us into Jesus' presence. Now, spiritual practices have been around forever, so this idea is not new. However, many of the traditional spiritual practices tend to be exercises for the mind alone and discount or even disconnect us from our bodies. If we look at what Jesus taught and the ways the early Christians engaged their bodies in their faith, we see that our bodies—and how we surrender and meet God in embodied ways—are important to him. Jesus touched bodies. He healed bodies. Our bodies matter in the living out of our relationship with him.

Absolute and final healing awaits us when God's Kingdom has fully come. After all, even those who were healed by Jesus' own hands eventually died and may have suffered again from bodily breakdowns and illnesses. In the same way, the healing we find now will be partial and temporary, and it may not look the way we want or expect it to. But we can trust that what God begins in us—transformation, healing, and freedom—he will complete (Philippians 1:6). So what we're going to do together, in pursuit of what his healing looks like here and now, is explore some spiritual practices that seek to bring our whole selves—and particularly the things we're not proud of—into Jesus' presence.

Perhaps you resonate with some or all of these very human conditions—brokenness, shame, anxiety, and fear—or maybe you've picked up this book to help "a friend." Either way, you might want to get under a blanket, curl up in your most comfortable spot, and wrap your hands around a favorite mug. You are receiving, right in this moment, an invitation into holy vulnerability.

Holy means set apart for God's purposes. *Vulnerability* means susceptibility to harm or attack. To enter into holy vulnerability, then, is to intentionally open ourselves to the possibility of harm in order for God to heal and mend and transform. Think of the humiliation which the paralyzed man and the bleeding woman decided to open themselves to. When we choose holy vulnerability, we present ourselves to our loving Father without our walls, protective gear, usual defenses, or bandages and allow him to begin to mend the broken parts of us, replace our fears with love, expose our shame for the lie that it is, and fill us with unshakable peace.

In normal life, we seek to avoid vulnerability at all costs. In fact, as author Daniel Taylor notes, "the great bulk of human activity of every kind aims at lessening [our] vulnerability."[1] Quite often, this is because we haven't let God come into the deepest parts of ourselves, where the imperfect and dark and hurt parts of us hide. Richard Rohr, writer and founder of the Center for Action and Contemplation, calls this "'the inner room' where Jesus invites us, and where things hide 'secretly' (Matthew 6:6)."[2]

Why do we guard this inner room with such vigilance? It's vulnerable, and vulnerability reminds us of our mortality, our inability to sustain ourselves, and the reality that we are not as indestructible as we pretend to be. In our culture, vulnerability equals weakness, and weakness exposes us in ways we find unacceptable. Indeed, we have all already been hurt in our lives back when we had no ability to protect ourselves and, for whatever reasons, those charged with our care could not or did not keep us from harm.

At first, holy vulnerability is a scary place. You might

feel alone and exposed. Few people are willing to dip a toe in these waters, let alone dive in headfirst. So, why would we allow ourselves to be open to such harm? And why would we do it intentionally?

We each have hurts that are so far down, so embedded, so delicate and sensitive that we can hardly bear the idea of ever allowing them to surface. And this is to say nothing of the pain that is so buried we could not name it even if we tried. But when our wounds are unbandaged, exposed, and examined in the presence of our loving God—Father, Son, and Spirit—they can be healed. Jesus is beckoning you into a place where you will ultimately come to feel at home, safe and cared for, loved and whole.

To say yes to the invitation into holy vulnerability requires emotional courage. As you walk around in it, you may feel a need to escape and return to where you feel it is safe. Reliving traumatic experiences, confronting failures, and sitting in the discomfort of shame, anxiety, and fear can be agonizing and exhausting. And so, as you enter into holy vulnerability, let me be the first to say, "It's okay. Take a break." Be gentle with yourself as you would with a close friend. God's invitation doesn't expire.

The alternative to holy vulnerability is unholy leakage. You know, that thing that happens when you are afraid, ashamed, or anxious, and instead of facing the reality of what you're experiencing, you just kind of spill it on everyone around you—usually your spouse, kids, or closest friends. Words intended to be lighthearted strike a sore spot, and an intimate dinner becomes a battlefield. An impending trip to your childhood home or family triggers anxiety that turns into unexplained impatience with your kids. An encounter with your scale or mirror or pair of jeans sends you into a spiral of withdrawal and self-hatred. An unknown hurt compels you to engage in well-worn destructive behaviors that you end up regretting.

Together, we're going to map a path out of unholy leakage and into holy vulnerability—and that path is through intentional spiritual practices that open us to God's work. I'm hoping that when you hear "spiritual practices for the broken, ashamed, anxious, and afraid," you feel something deep within you nodding in agreement, saying, *Yes. That is me. I want to meet God in the middle of my pain. These practices aren't for the spiritually elite—they're for me.* But I also want to clarify: When I say "broken, ashamed, anxious, and afraid," I am pointing to the aspects of these things that we all experience as part of the human condition. Many people are dealing with more severe manifestations that require significant professional help or recovery programs; I myself have needed counseling and medication for anxiety at various points. Needing that kind of intervention in no way reflects weakness of faith or determination or anything else. I'm not offering medical opinions; I'm speaking to the struggles that run through all our lives and where God longs to meet us in them.

So here's where we're going in this book. In Part I, we'll start by learning to notice where it seems God is absent and brokenness is breaking in. Where is anxiety occupying our hearts and minds; fear hindering our relationships, faith, and joy; shame causing us to question our self-worth? We'll gently examine the ways we have come to cope when we experience anxiety, fear, shame, and brokenness—and how these coping practices affect us and our families and friends.

In Part II, we'll explore six different spiritual practices intended to open us to God's healing and transformation. These practices may not be what you expect or what you envision when you think about intentional spiritual work. But I assure you—as we step out in holy vulnerability, God will meet us there. These practices aren't for those ubermature people who have it all together and have gaping holes in their daily schedules. They are for us, people in the middle of stuff with families and jobs and difficult stories. They are designed to help us penetrate the illusions we have and get in touch with what is real.[3]

As I mentioned briefly above, one thing to know about the practices we're going to explore together is that they are bodily—in other words, they require something more than thinking. They require action, and as you go along, the amount of action they require increases. This is on purpose because the more our bodies are involved, the more fully we are offering ourselves to God for his healing and transformation. All the practices may not hold equal weight for you. Some may come more naturally than others—in which case, I'd say move on to those that feel like you're writing with your nondominant hand because the stuff that comes naturally doesn't stretch us much. But when you feel weary, return to the ones that feel more natural. Also, depending on the season you're currently in, some of the practices may seem really helpful, but almost like they're for a later time. I once attended a retreat that began with the question "How many of you are exhausted?" Every hand in the room but mine shot up. I happened to be in a season that felt manageable and restful. The practices we learned were about recuperating, making space for rest, and learning to be content in silence and solitude. None felt particularly relevant to me at the time, but I knew I'd need them at some point, so I dove in and reminded myself that these were going to come in handy one day. The practices I learned during that retreat have been bringing me life and peace in God's presence ever since.

If your soul thirsts for God and longs to be taken into his presence, join me. The journey into holy vulnerability and away from unholy leakage is not easy, but it's what we need. We were made to be in and can flourish in God's presence, so even in this time in history where sin and hurt still abound, there is goodness and healing and rest when we open ourselves and accept Jesus' invitation to come and drink.

Father, our healer, we need you. Allow us to know your presence as we move into the places of deep vulnerability in our lives. We hold so much in our bodies and hearts and minds. Give us the courage to walk with you and expose these places to you for healing. Be gentle and kind to us—and most of all, grant us the privilege of encountering you.

PART I

NOTICING OUR ABSENCE

❁entistry has come a long way since I was a child. Back then, in search of cavities from all the Mike and Ikes I ate, my dentist would probe my teeth for soft spots with a scary metal, hooked tool (which I've since learned is called a sickle probe). Then, based on his experience and best guess about what he was feeling, he would decide whether I needed a filling. These days, dentists are a lot more precise. A laser tool measures density and weakness in the tooth, and a sufficiently high reading indicates that there's enough decay to warrant a filling.

No matter the method, the reality is still the same:

Living with decayed teeth is painful. But we can't identify the decay, remove it, and insert a filling ourselves by the power of our will, with the help of a dentistry book, or with our own set of tools. There is no do-it-yourself fix. We have to go to a dentist to remove the decay and find relief from the pain. Only a dentist can drill out the bad parts and fill the gap with something better so that we can still use our teeth.

Even though dental decay can be debilitating, we're not naturally inclined to go looking for decay and proactively root it out before it becomes a huge problem. So many of us hate going to the dentist—most commonly because of the feelings of vulnerability and helplessness that come from having someone using sharp instruments near our life-giving airways as we sit motionless in a chair, unable to participate in any way in our own care.[1]

But if we really think about it, dental care isn't the only part of life where we're apprehensive about allowing ourselves to be probed for decay. Anytime someone points out our weaknesses, especially those we don't seem to have much control over, we feel attacked. We feel vulnerable and helpless. We're tempted to avoid the conversation, to shut down and decline the invitation to look closer at the decay.

We've all got places of decay in our bodies, hearts, and minds—and we all are tempted to turn to avoidance tactics and coping mechanisms to avoid the vulnerability of addressing them. We may see the signs of a problem, but we close our eyes, endure the pain, or find ways to work around it. But the thing about decay is that when we don't address it, the pain just gets more intense. The damage gets worse. We don't have a chance of getting healthy until we decide to face where things are rotting within us.

How can we begin to notice when our brokenness harms us or others, when shame tears apart our insides, anxiety preoccupies and distracts, and fear inhibits and prevents the fullness of life Jesus came to bring? How can we slow down enough to discover the places within us that are full of decay? We must start with our need and then be willing to face the painful ways it manifests itself in our lives.

CHAPTER I

NOTICING OUR NEED

*We are infinite souls inside finite lives and that alone should
be enough to explain our incessant and insatiable aching.*

RONALD ROLHEISER

$\mathscr{B}$efore I met Jesus, I thought I had everything pretty much together. I moved from high school to college to law school to a successful legal career with aplomb—a very astute manager of my world, in my opinion. I wasn't perfect, sure, but I considered myself fairly capable of navigating around anything that would keep me from being the kind of person I wanted to be, living the kind of life I wanted to live.

But then, unexpectedly, my well-worn ways of controlling my own particular idiosyncrasies and temptations, as I would have called them then, stopped working. I began to see what I knew to be wrong as necessary for my own well-being, the only way to emotionally survive. This subconscious shift was immensely destructive. And I wasn't living in this place of desolation for a few weeks. I spent *ten years* trying to make what felt like a broken life work. It took me ten years to realize I needed help.

When it seemed I had no personal capacity left, nothing more to draw on within myself, I cried out to God—and as he does, "he turned to me and heard my cry. He lifted me out of the pit of despair, out of the mud and the mire. He set my feet on solid ground and steadied me as I walked along" (Psalm 40:1-2). This is not an uncommon human compulsion—to cry out to God when we are desperate, when we have no other options. As Richard Rohr says, "until and unless there is a person, situation, event, idea, conflict, or relationship that you cannot 'manage,' you will never find the True Manager."[1]

When I turned to God, I stepped down as manager, as best as I knew how, and gave my life over to Jesus. At the time, this looked like a complete turnaround. My interests changed, the kinds of books I read shifted, my thoughts became less self-focused, and the people I wanted to be around reflected the values of this new life. God gently showed me how and equipped me to turn away from the destructive habits and behaviors that had plagued me. During this time, I had very little fear or anxiety, I did not seem as tempted as I had been, and I was sure that whatever had been broken was (mostly) healed. I seemed to be hearing from the Lord on a daily basis. I was emboldened to love and serve, to give my time and my money. I encountered God in tangible and unforgettable ways. As far as I could tell, God had full access.

But then, after a number of years, something changed. Not all that was broken within me, I realized, had been fully healed. Some cracks still existed. Some old susceptibilities still presented themselves from time to time. Fear found a place again. Anxious thoughts returned. My brokenness seemed less dramatic and obvious than it had been before I called out to God—and in that way, perhaps more difficult to identify—but still there. My destructive patterns became subtler and less obvious, something that is common according to spiritual writers who call these more disguised sins "the faults of those already advanced beyond first conversion."[2] These are the sins we excuse as "not that bad" or "just part of our personality."

Over time, God's voice, once so clear and ever-present in my days, had quieted. With each passing year, I feel a deeper longing for the old days, the days just after my conversion when I felt so alive and on fire. I think I may have stepped back in as manager, resumed my position as CEO, and then found myself having closed God out. I didn't decide to turn away from God or wrest control back. This change happened over time, as I slowly turned inward and became undisciplined about practicing my faith in an outward sense. My faith became primarily an internal, intellectual endeavor. My perspective, outward and others-focused in my early days of faith, had turned back toward myself. And when I stopped to pay attention, I realized that this self-focus coincided with (caused?) my resurgence of anxiety and fear.

That is the first step in inviting God into our places of brokenness, shame, anxiety, and fear: noticing. Where are we sensing an absence, that feeling we've taken back control and subconsciously asked God to step aside? Where are we experiencing unholy leakage, the spilling over of attitudes and behaviors that eat away at our hearts and our relationships with others?

We've got to open our eyes to these conditions we carry. We cannot make ourselves available to God as healer and Savior without acknowledging that we are in need, and that our need has a name. And remember, *our needs are not our identity*. Noticing the reality that I am broken, ashamed, anxious, and afraid doesn't mean I am only those things. Our God-given self-worth holds even when we acknowledge our need.

NEEDY AND BROKEN

Not long ago, my husband and I cared for a little girl named Mary[3] who had been removed from her home because she'd been abused and neglected by her parents—the people entrusted to care for and love this gift they'd been given. She was in poor health, having neither gone to the doctor since she was born nor visited the dentist in her life. Her parents were addicted to opiods and left their apartment dirty and dangerous. Mary talked about things like going to jail, getting into trouble, and feeling pain in her private parts. Her body was covered with scrapes and bruises. She couldn't return home and had no one related to her that could take her in.

Things are not as they should be. Thousands upon thousands of children have stories like Mary's. Children are abused, exploited, neglected, trafficked. And while we may say we aren't as bad as those who abuse the innocent, darkness lingers within each of us. We feel rage toward that coworker who is dismissive toward us; we are tempted to lie to cover our tracks; we get angry at that one commentator on our Facebook posts or the driver that cuts us off; we resent people who require our time and attention; and we grow bitter and envious when others succeed. We know that something is fundamentally wrong with both the world outside of us and with what is going on inside of us. I don't think this proposition is truly in question, though it seems, as theologian Cornelius Plantinga notes, "where sin is concerned, people mumble now."[4] Indeed, even saying the word *sin* today can provoke both confusion and accusations of judgmentalism. But we can't get very far in our quest to open ourselves to God's presence and healing without talking about sin.

In our post-postmodern world, however, the word *sin* no longer carries immediate understanding. I like using the words *broken* or *brokenness* instead, not because they remove culpability but because few people, even in our secular world, can claim to not understand what it means to be broken. We all know when something is not working as it was intended.

Brokenness encompasses wrongs we commit, rights we omit, and the general state of a world in which children get cancer, tornadoes and landslides kill entire communities, and famine destroys an entire generation. Brokenness doesn't mean those things that seem to impinge on our well-being or mental health, like being unable to find a parking spot, walking the grocery cart all the way back to the store's front door, or having our opinion go unheard. The fact that we must exert effort or even fail at certain tasks does not reflect that sin is at work or that the world is not as it should be. But our reaction, whether internal or external, to the situations and obstacles we face may indeed provide evidence of this reality.

Of course, brokenness is more than things that happen to us; we are quite culpable much of the time. There's no end to what our pride, selfishness, and wounds can motivate us to do, say, or think. And we can really be hard on ourselves when we see our sins. We are good at self-condemnation. We are great at heaping shame on ourselves to the point where we close God out, not wanting to be seen in our messy state.

Cornelius Plantinga defines sin as "culpable shalom-breaking,"[5] and being far more experienced in committing sin than defining it, I find his definition the best to use here. By shalom, Plantinga means "the way things ought to be," or more richly stated, "universal flourishing, whole-ness, and delight."[6] So if sin is culpable shalom-breaking, brokenness is the absence of shalom inside or outside of ourselves, whether we specifically are blameworthy or not.

It's certainly easier for most of us to see what's wrong "out there" and point the sickle probe at others than it is to allow ourselves to be open to God (or others) and iden-tify our personal areas of decay. Jesus spoke directly to this human tendency: "How can you think of saying to your friend, 'Let me help you get rid of that speck in your eye,' when you can't see past the log in your own eye?" (Matthew 7:4). Also, we humans tend to live with an everlasting opti-mism (naiveté?) that we are capable of fixing what's wrong if only we can find the right book, program, practices, or steps or if enough good-intentioned people participate. We think that if we try hard enough, we can will away (or even explain away) our rebellion, selfishness, and defensiveness. These thought processes are a denial of the reality in which we live. No objective arbiter would look at the evidence of human history and conclude, "Yes, if they would just try harder, all the problems of the world would be solved."

I recently watched a movie about a couple who moved from a small city apartment to a large piece of land, intending to start a "traditional" farm where all would be in harmony. What they discovered instead was that with each positive introduction to their farm—peach trees, or chickens, or a pond—a new pest or problem would arise. Solving one problem (growing ground cover in the orchard to ensure softer, more productive soil) led to a new problem (snails thriving in the ground cover and devouring the peach trees). As I watched, I couldn't help thinking, *This is what we do!* When a problem creeps up, we seek to solve it—and our solution only causes another problem. I take medication for my generalized anxiety, and the medication has worked so well in helping minimize my anxiety that I want to write a letter to the manufacturer. But there are side effects—one of which is night sweats. Solve one problem, and another finds a foothold.

We may feel a bit hopeless in the face of this idea that our brokenness is unsolvable by us and that, while we may make great progress toward wholeness, something else will always creep up. Yet here is the greater hope: Throughout Scripture, God invites us to turn to him in our brokenness (and sin), not away. Jesus said more about forgiveness, healing, and life than he ever did about sin and brokenness. As C. S. Lewis explains, what God often "first helps us towards is not the virtue itself but just this power of always trying again. For however important [a particular virtue] may be, this process trains us in habits of the soul which are more important still. It cures our illusions about ourselves and teaches us to depend on God."[7] So what if we took God up on his invitation? What if we said yes to his help and his gracious and restorative presence?

At the end of the day, God's intervention in our brokenness is why we're Christians. We realize the direness of our situation and find our only hope in Jesus Christ. So yes, let us observe our brokenness and sin with sorrow. But what if we also examine it with curiosity instead of self-condemnation? What if we could view ourselves with the graciousness we might offer a friend under similar circumstances? What if we could turn to God even in the midst of temptation and in the depths of our brokenness?

NEEDY AND ASHAMED

Shame is often tied closely to our brokenness. We tend to feel it based on immoral or hurtful things we have done or awful things that have been done to us that we feel, wrongly, responsible for. I should be an expert on shame. I have a lot of it. Shame causes me to almost hate myself for merely being human—for being imperfect, saying the wrong thing or something unkind, being incapable of overcoming my fear of flying, getting older and changing shape, making mistakes, wanting to blame others for my own failures or insecurities, and on and on. Instead of seeing mistakes or imperfection as part of the human (and thus my) condition, I see them as evidence that I am fundamentally and unchangeably defective.

Brené Brown, an actual expert on shame,[8] defines shame this way: "the intensely painful feeling or experience of believing that we are flawed and therefore unworthy of love and belonging."[9] To be honest, when I read this definition for the first time, it didn't really resonate with me. At the time, I would have said that shame isn't a struggle I have. But here is what I have learned: Shame is something we all have, just in differing degrees and under different circumstances. Brené Brown identifies twelve categories of shame that she has seen in her research: appearance and body image; money and work; motherhood/fatherhood; family; parenting; mental and physical health; addiction; sex; aging; religion; surviving trauma; and being stereotyped or labeled.[10] We've probably all had shame around some or all of these categories, though it seems it's usually one or two that can really send us into a downward spiral.

In the Bible, shame first comes to life in Genesis 3:7, when Adam and Eve's eyes are opened and they realize they are naked. Some translations specifically say they felt shame (NLT), and commentators argue that awareness of their nakedness brought them shame.[11] Why? They did what God, who wanted only their ultimate good and flourishing, specifically told them not to do. This sin forged a rift between them and God, causing them to discover the vulnerability and weakness of being human apart from God.

When we are ashamed, we feel this same relational break with God and others. Shame makes us believe there is something fundamentally wrong with us that will cause others to reject us. It makes us believe we are bad and unworthy of love and belonging. But sin and shame are not the same. When Adam and Eve sinned, there were consequences. Their intimate communion with God had been broken. Yet they were not unloved or unlovable. After all, God made them garments to cover their nakedness, blessed them with children, and sustained them (Genesis 3:21–4:26).

The foundation of shame is this: When we act or speak or think in a way we shouldn't, the accusing voices we have in our minds—the shame "gremlins," as Brené Brown refers to them[12]—don't stick with the reality of "you did a terrible thing." Instead, they accuse, "You're a terrible person." Shame picks us apart and makes our lack or failure our identity.

But shame doesn't just limit itself to personal, internal attacks. I also encounter what seems to be a subtler, maybe more insidious kind of gremlin: the one that says "*she* is a terrible person" or "*he* is the one that's not parenting well." One of my most prominent areas of brokenness is that I am judgmental—way more than I feel comfortable admitting. I tend to keep my judgmentalism out of sight, silently berating myself for the unwelcome thoughts, but every now and then it sneaks out in a sideways, snarky comment or in a look.

Lately I've been exploring where this tendency comes from and if it rears its head at certain times more than others. My husband asked me a question that has stuck with me, one that I think explains a lot: "Have you always been this critical of yourself?" I don't remember what I'd said to prompt his inquiry, but it was obviously some kind of veiled (or not) criticism of myself. Something in that conversation made me realize I *am* really critical of myself. But I take this self-criticism—my own shame—and project it onto others. Let's say I think, *I never see so-and-so read her Bible. I bet she never does.* But really, I've hit a slump in my own Bible reading. I've told myself I "should" read the Bible every day. And, the logic follows, I'm a bad Christian because I'm in a slump. To avoid feeling the pain of this reality or extending myself compassion, I project this judgment onto someone else. Brené Brown notes,

> What's ironic (or perhaps natural) is that research tells us that we judge people in areas where we're vulnerable to shame, especially picking folks who are doing worse than we're doing. If I feel good about my parenting, I have no interest in judging other people's choices. If I feel good about my body, I don't go around making fun of other people's weight or appearance. We're hard on each other because we're using each other as a launching pad out of our own perceived shaming deficiency.[13]

The undercurrent of shame in many of our lives is so common we don't always notice it. But shame does not have to rule us or become our identity—if we are willing to open ourselves to God's presence in the midst of our shame. After all, Jesus came into the world to save it and release us from the hold of sin and shame. At its core, shame is the fear that we are flawed and unworthy of love or belonging. In Jesus, though, we can call shame what it is: a lie. As Paul says so powerfully in his letter to the

Christians in Rome: "So now there is no condemnation for those who belong to Christ Jesus" (Romans 8:1).

NEEDY AND ANXIOUS

Anxiety is an old, very loyal friend of mine. I'm not sure exactly when we met, but it was early in my life. On my first day of kindergarten, when I was five, the school-bus driver dropped me off by myself at my own empty house instead of at the babysitter's. I don't remember much, except that I was crying and made the decision to walk to my baby-sitter's house, miles away. As I walked along the side of the street in our neighborhood, tears streaming down my face, a man pulled up in a car and asked if I was lost. I refused to speak with him and continued walking. He was persistent and told me where he lived (he was a neighbor) and that he wanted to help me find my parents. After a lot of coaxing, I agreed to follow behind his car to his house and to stand at the bottom of the driveway so he and his wife could call my mom. (There were no cell phones back then.) I didn't know the name of the company where my mom worked, but I knew she worked for a lawyer named Jack. Since we lived in a relatively small town, the neighbors were eventually able to get ahold of my mom using the yellow pages.

About a year later—in a series of events unrelated to this incident—my parents got divorced. And, although anxiety may be a result of many factors (such as heredity, biology, family background and upbringing, conditioning, recent life changes, and environmental stressors[14]), I feel confident that my terrifying first day of school and my parents' divorce have played a major role in my life with anxiety. Since those early years of my life, I've lived with a sense of instability and worry about whether things are fundamentally okay in the world and whether I am safe. My general operating system tells me that nothing is secure and that anything is liable to fall apart, shift, or disappear at any moment. I have an ever-present sense of dread or foreboding, and I tend to catastrophize in my own mind. All of this comes so naturally that I didn't realize until recently that it was out of the ordinary or had a name (generalized anxiety disorder or free-floating anxiety).[15]

Anxiety is a whole-being experience—"it is a physiological, behavioral, and psychological reaction all at once."[16] Physically, I'm rarely at ease. My stomach is almost always tight, my jaw's natural state is tense, and my hands sweat. I have frequent headaches, and when my anxiety is at its worst, I hyperventilate. As I write this, I feel ashamed that my mind and body are defective in these ways and am worried about what you think of me, how what I'm writing may influence any future jobs I seek, and what effect my words could have on insurance coverage down the road. (See what I mean about catastrophizing?) Another thing: Shame only magnifies anxiety.[17] If ever there were a place I need God, it is here, in this anxiety-shame-more-anxiety cycle.

But the most frustrating aspect of my anxiety is that I have a hard time connecting with God in the midst of it.

I can't seem to raise myself out of my spinning thoughts, gain a broader perspective, or even open myself to the possibility that God can be present with me during these panicky moments or seasons. Anxiety causes a kind of tunnel vision and self-focus that can feel impossible to get out of. I have tried to follow the advice of the apostle Peter, who said, "Cast all your anxiety on him because he cares for you" (1 Peter 5:7, NIV). But I don't know how to get ahold of my anxiety in order to then cast it elsewhere. I have internalized Jesus' words not to worry and his reminder that a single day can't be added to my life through worrying (Matthew 6:25-34). Unfortunately, as true as I know these words to be, I can't seem to follow them. Deciding not to worry or willing myself to stop feeling anxious doesn't work. As philosopher Dallas Willard observed, "No one can succeed in mastering feelings in his or her life who tries to simply take them head-on and resist or redirect them by 'willpower' in the moment of choice."[18]

Still, I don't think Jesus or Peter (and others in Scripture) were asking us to do the impossible. When they gave these instructions, they had a whole-person experience in mind, one involving the mind and the body, one bound by relationship and trust. Jesus spoke his words about worry in his Sermon on the Mount, a teaching that illustrates a life devoted to God and marked by complete trust in his care and provision. Peter tells us to cast our anxiety on God only *after* he tells us to humble ourselves under God's mighty power.

NEEDY AND AFRAID

I'm sure you've heard or read that in Scripture, God tells us not to be afraid 365 times—once for every day of the year.[19] Whenever someone posts this on social media or shares it in a group setting, I can't help but wonder at its helpfulness. Or, to be more direct: I don't find it helpful and, in fact, find it shaming. Fear doesn't magically turn into peace upon the instruction, "Do not be afraid." And being afraid isn't something we can control by simply thinking differently: Our bodies have built-in mechanisms that kick into gear before our minds even know we're afraid.

There are a lot of things to be afraid of these days. As I write, virtually the whole world is "sheltered at home"— required to stay home except to get essentials like toilet paper, medicine, and food—because of the rapid spread of COVID-19. Except for the very few who were alive during the Spanish flu epidemic in 1918, none of us has experienced anything like this before. For all our technological, medicinal, and social progress, we are still walking around in mortal, susceptible, vulnerable bodies. To protect our bodies right now, we have to stay away from other people, lest we catch or spread a virus that has the power to kill in a matter of days. We won't know how bad things are or could have been for many years, I'm sure, but this *is* scary and worthy of fear. And this is just one example.

But how do we hold the tension between the ever-present fear around us and God's daily admonition not to be afraid? Is that really what it is?

Like brokenness, shame, and anxiety, fear is part of what it is to be human. We are afraid of endless things, from the very understandable to the bizarre. Our fears can generally be categorized into five types: fear of no longer existing (of which fear of death is a part); fear of being hurt or having our bodies invaded in some way (think snakes, spiders, needles, the dentist); fear of powerlessness or the loss of freedom (think suffocation, drowning, imprisonment, aging); fear of rejection or abandonment; and fear of humiliation or shame.[20]

I first encountered debilitating fear when I was a junior in high school. In religion class, we were reading a book about life's big questions, and while I don't remember which question was raised, I do remember zoning out pretty suddenly as I realized that one day I would not only die but not exist. The fear that gripped me was like nothing I've ever felt before or since. I was overcome by a foreboding sense of utter nothingness. My life was headed toward absence, despair. I couldn't pull myself out of the panic I felt. My heart raced, my hands became sweaty, and I felt dizzy and nauseous. I thought I might faint. Even though I was in a Catholic school, I didn't consider—until much later in my life—that there might be a scenario in which life waited for me on the other side of death.

Is fear something we can overcome—and should overcoming fear even be our goal? We all have undoubtedly heard stories of people conquering fears, and we may have even done so ourselves. The psalmist says God delivered him from all his fears (Psalm 34:4). And according to John, the one referred to as the apostle Jesus loved (John 13:23; 19:26), "perfect love expels all fear" (1 John 4:18). But in my experience, fear isn't something I can ever fully shake. I thought I had overcome my fear of flying in the mid-2000s, when I flew constantly for work; the more I flew, the less afraid I was. But the fear returned with a vengeance as I began to fly less and less.

While I'd like to be fearless, I'm not sure that lack of fear alone is the goal. When I look at the passages of Scripture about fear, I see something different from an instruction to knuckle down and overcome. God's Word doesn't seem to order us to use human efforts to banish fear. I see instead an invitation to trust, to be present, and to be aware of God's presence where we might otherwise assume his absence:

> Psalm 23:4: [David wrote,] "Even when I walk through the darkest valley, I will not be afraid, *for you are close beside me*."

> Joshua 1:9: [The Lord said,] "This is my command—be strong and courageous! Do not be afraid or discouraged. For *the LORD your God is with you* wherever you go."

> Deuteronomy 31:6: [Moses said,] "Be strong and courageous! Do not be afraid and do not panic

before them [the nations living in Canaan]. *For the
LORD your God will personally go ahead of you. He
will neither fail you nor abandon you."*

1 Chronicles 28:20: [David said,] "Be strong and
courageous, and do the work. Don't be afraid or
discouraged, *for the LORD God, my God, is with you.
He will not fail you or forsake you."*

Isaiah 41:10: [The Lord said,] "Don't be afraid,
for I am with you. Don't be discouraged, for I am
your God."[21]

This is the confidence we have from Scripture: The
more we live into the reality of God's presence, the more
aware we are of him, the more we embrace his love for
us—the less of a hold fear will have on us. Why is this so?
Because God himself, in and through Jesus Christ, conquered our deepest fears and has opened the pathway into
dependence on his love. We can trust him because of not
only what we see in Jesus but also what God did through
Jesus: He came in human flesh to demonstrate God's love;
he lived the life of a perfect human to show us what total
trust in God looks like; he died on the cross to atone for
the sin of all humanity; God raised him from the dead to
display his power over the scariest thing of all: death; and
he ascended to the right hand of the Father, alive, promis-
ing to bring us there with him—alive—in the end. Left by

ourselves and to our own capabilities, there are plenty of things to be afraid of in this world. But God is not shaking a finger at us and telling us to try harder to not be afraid. He is telling us that as we lean into him and trust him, our fear will dissipate.

BEING CURIOUS

How can we notice when our brokenness is at play? Or when our shame is causing us to act in harmful ways? How do we notice when anxiety and fear are dictating our words, thoughts, or behaviors? Like so many other things, noticing these parts of ourselves is a process that takes intention and reflection.

Noticing, very simply, is paying attention; it's being curious about how we move through life and why we respond the way we do. I can't always distinguish between and among brokenness, shame, anxiety, and fear, but if I'm paying attention, I start to notice when something in my internal or external responses feels off.

A key phrase I've learned in my noticing is "hysterical = historical." I'm not sure where this comes from or who coined it first, but in essence, it means that when you have a strong (over)reaction to something, your response probably has some connection to another event or experience in your life that was hurtful, made you feel misunderstood, or caused you distress. Of course, sometimes you might just be passionate about a particular issue, but strong reactions can be a signal of brokenness, shame, anxiety, or fear. Noticing a disproportionate response allows us to get curious about what's causing it.

I've also learned to look out for defensiveness. For example, let's say that our garage door starts having issues over the weekend, and my husband and I agree we should call someone to fix it during the week. I have more free time in my schedule on Monday, so we also agree I'll make the call. But when Monday comes, I completely forget to call. That evening, my husband asks me, "Did you ever call about the garage?" An innocent enough question, right? He's just checking in on something we talked about previously. But I immediately get defensive and respond in an irritated tone, "We *just* talked about it yesterday." (Translated: "I can't believe you're asking me already. I'm a busy person, and I've been working on other things. I'm not lazy!") I don't say, "Oh, oops, I forgot. I'll put it on my list for tomorrow." Instead, I get angry about being asked at all. Unholy leakage.

That particular unholy leakage leads me to even more: spiraling. A few minutes after that kind of defensive inter- action, I start berating myself for forgetting. I look back on my day and see all the times I could have called but didn't; I consider my lack of responsibility; and I feel embar- rassed for saying I'd do something and then failing to do it. Spiraling is another signal. Shame has taken hold. A minor mistake runs through my mind nonstop, leading to fear and uncertainty about my worth.

Lastly, gut feelings can be a helpful prompting. Even

in our day, when so much seems permissible, we all know when we've acted out of bounds—when we snapped at a coworker or were passive-aggressive toward a friend. Our own conscience makes us aware, and if we are Christians, the Holy Spirit has a way of convicting our hearts when we've done something sinful.

I don't always notice when I'm acting out of brokenness, shame, anxiety, or fear. These things can be so deeply rooted that, while I sense something's going on, I'm not always sure what. Sometimes I am really impatient or anxious or short with others without any sense of why. Noticing the subtler, deeper, disguised, and well-worn areas of brokenness, shame, anxiety, and fear can be far more difficult. But that's when we can take a closer look at a key signal of those deeper struggles: our coping practices. That's what we'll talk about next.

But we shouldn't try to suppress our feelings or forget about them and move along with our day. God wants to be invited into our brokenness, our anxiety and shame and fear. We need God in these places. So when we sense a part of our lives where we have pushed him out or not allowed him in, let's not power through or shut down or avoid a closer look. Let's get curious. Ignoring or dealing with these conditions on our own steals our peace and joy; self-dependence blocks the full life that Jesus came to give. But dependence, inviting God into the parts of ourselves we don't understand, creates opportunities to encounter him. And if the Bible is true, to encounter God is better even than the healing he might bring to a particular issue. Ultimately, whatever underlies our brokenness, shame, anxiety, and fear can be satisfied by God's loving presence.

REFLECTION QUESTIONS

1. In what area(s) of your life does God seem absent or feel distant to you? In what area(s) do you long for God's presence?

2. Consider the ways in which you feel your brokenness, shame, anxiety, and fear internally. What comes to mind? Notice any overlap between your answers to this question and your answers to the first question.

3. How does brokenness manifest itself outwardly in your life? What about shame? Anxiety? Fear?

4. Which of the four conditions we've talked about do you experience the most? Which do you experience the least? Which is most foreign to you altogether? About which one(s) might you say, "I don't struggle with that"?

5. In what area(s) of your life are you most longing for healing?

CHAPTER 2

RECOGNIZING OUR COPING PRACTICES

The sin of man consists in that he does not want to be flesh.

HERMAN RIDDERBOS

The gate agent called for Group 8 to board. I swung my backpack over my shoulder, grabbed my water bottle, and got in line with others who would ride through the sky together for the next eight or nine hours—first to Ethiopia, and then another eight or nine hours to Ndola, Zambia. When I found my window seat, I settled in and waited. A man sat next to me in the middle seat—poor guy—and I immediately wondered where his backpack was. He had no book, no bag, no headphones, no nothing—just his boarding pass in his hands. I started to worry that the flight would be delayed because he had obviously left his bag in the terminal. We would all pay for his forgetfulness when he realized it and ran down the aisle, asking the flight attendant to hold the door. I glanced a few times down to the empty space at his feet, thinking that might spark his memory, but he didn't make a move. The doors closed, and the words "cross-check," "pushback," and "seat belt" came over the loudspeaker. *How disappointing*, I thought, *it would be to leave a bag and spend the early parts of your trip trying to get it back.*

"You didn't forget your bag, did you?" I could not help myself (I worry for other people too). The man looked at me, a bit startled by the question.

"Uh, no. I've got everything." He smiled. "Light traveler."

Light traveler. Apparently so. I, however, was not—and began unpacking for the ride. I had a whole routine that I had pretty much mastered, having flown all over the world for many years. First, I got out my noise-cancelling headphones and curled them around my neck. Next, I unsnapped my squishy neck pillow from its place on the outside of the backpack and put that on the armrest next to me. I tucked my phone under my thigh and pulled out my iPad, which I had loaded up with five movies and three television shows the night before. I never knew what I would be in the mood for—something new, an old faithful, an action-adventure with sharks or dinosaurs, or an intense drama. Of course, my iPad also held books that I might want along the way—fiction, nonfiction, poetry, essays, and short stories. But I also had my fiction library book in case I wanted something fairly light. I pulled a small bottle out of the side-zippered section of my bag and slid a little yellow pill into my front pocket. I grabbed my glasses and a set of my disposable contacts out of the other side section and put both in the seat pocket in front of me. When it was time to sleep, I would take out my contacts so they wouldn't dry up in my eyes (otherwise, I would need a new pair after waking up). The glasses were necessary in case I needed to actually see anything during the no-contact period.

I was nearing the end of my preparation period when I noticed the man next to me was watching all this unfold. He looked impressed, and I felt on top of things. I was in control. And then I had a revelation that would stick with me for months—a revelation that I feel confident struck everyone other than me within a few seconds of watching (or reading through) this routine. I had all these things with me not to pass the time on the flight; I had them as a way of coping with my fear of flying, and more to the point, my fear of dying. I pushed my backpack under the seat in front of me and shook my head. I started to imagine what it would be like to fly with none of this stuff I had brought with me so faithfully over the years. What if I brought nothing but my boarding pass on board? I don't think I'd survive. Really. The thought of not having my headphones, my yellow pill, all my movies and books, and my neck pillow triggered panic.

I thought of the story I had heard many years earlier

about John Wesley, founder of the Methodist denomination. In 1735, he and his brother were on a ship traveling to America as missionaries of the Anglican Church. The ship passed through a terrible storm that threatened to sink the ship. In the midst of what must have been a chaotic scene, a group of immigrants, who were part of the Moravian church, sang worship songs and praised God with abandon. Meanwhile, Wesley cowered in fear, terrified of death. When the storm finally subsided, Wesley asked one of the group of worshipers, "Were you not afraid?" The man answered that neither he nor any of the other men, women, or children were afraid to die.[1] Here Wesley was, a Christian missionary, and a very disciplined one at that, traveling across the ocean to share the gospel of Jesus Christ—but once he no longer felt in control, he no longer "trusted" God.[2]

I don't know if the guy sitting next to me on my cross-continental plane ride was a Christian or not. But here I was, a Christian pastor, flying across the globe to attend the funeral of my spiritual mentor and friend . . . and anxiety and fear had such a grip on me that I needed all kinds of gadgets and comforts to essentially trick my psyche into feeling safe. I felt ashamed and started to hear things in my brain like, *Where's your trust? What is your faith in? What are you afraid of?* And then, some other part of my brain would yell back, *Dying! I'm afraid of dying!* A quieter voice whispered, *I guess I don't trust you. I'm still afraid.* I wondered if John Wesley heard these same voices.

Not to state the obvious, but to be human is to be "in *time* and in the *body*."³ And maybe not so obviously, we all—whether we realize it or not—resent and rebel against these limitations, though they have been ours since the beginning. We all experience aging, sickness, and death. And we also experience little indignities like sore muscles, sweat, headaches, unpleasant odors, bad breath, sunburns, and unwanted weight gain. All these bodily limitations can be irritating. But often what we find even more frustrating is our lack of control. God has given us such freedom, intelligence, and power that we deny the undeniable: that we are not sovereign and we are not the center of the universe. As Cornelius Plantinga says, we fail to face the truth that we "have not made ourselves, cannot keep ourselves, cannot ultimately oblige or forgive ourselves."⁴ It is only in God that "we live and move and exist" (Acts 17:28). When our bodies remind us again of our weaknesses, limitations, and ultimately, our mortality, we can turn to God and seek what we lack. In other words, "our flesh creates a longing only He [God] can fulfill."⁵ But, more often than not, instead of turning to God when we sense these longings, we seek to fulfill them in other ways or try to escape or numb ourselves from feeling them at all. We may overeat, drink too much, binge-watch television shows, or seek to escape our thoughts through unhealthy levels of sexual gratification, exercise, or video games. We attempt to reassure and regulate ourselves by feeding the apparent needs of our bodies.

This impulse is not crazy. There is a connection between our bodies and our heart condition and our mental well-being. We recognize this intuitively. When we engage our bodies in healthy ways, something in us begins to heal. But when we attempt to use our bodies to regain a sense of control (where there actually is none), we push off healing and damage ourselves further.

Why is this? Because when we spin with worry, fear, and shame, we are living in a moment other than the present. We are not grounded and anchored in *what is*. With worry and fear, we are projecting our thoughts into the future and predicting what might happen. And when we are stuck in shame, we are stuck in the past, remembering and regretting what happened then. Similarly, when we give in to temptation (experiencing our own brokenness), we are allowing our past or our fears about the future to dictate our present.

The only moment that is fully real is our present, and when we are present in our bodies, we are present in the moment. The present is quite literally all we have, yet we are constantly seeking to escape it. The present is vulnerable, after all. But it is also the place we encounter ourselves fully—and the place in which we can encounter God. Brokenness, shame, anxiety, and fear all seem to respond when we open our minds *and* our bodies to God's presence and God's healing.

I feel a bit silly saying this, but I have the hardest time accepting all of this—that I'm human. It's as if my heart or body or some other unidentified part of me just doesn't get it or doesn't want to. I feel substantial shame when I make a minor mistake, and I'm embarrassed that my hands sweat when I'm hot or nervous—displaying the very human characteristic of imperfection. When I don't hear back from my daughter right away when I've texted her, anxiety hastens my breath, tightens my stomach, and catastrophizes my thoughts—I'm bumping into the truth that humans are not omnipotent. When I respond with irritation or judgment to something my husband says, hours and hours pass before I stop beating myself up about failing to muster the right response—I'm succumbing to the human trait of tiredness or pain.

Each of us has our own little idiosyncrasies that betray our inability to lean into our humanity. But as author Parker Palmer notes, "We can neither survive nor thrive until we embrace our human frailty with reverence and respect."[6] Or, as the apostle Paul puts it, "Do not think of yourself more highly than you ought" (Romans 12:3, NIV). This is so hard! As babies and small children, we are experts at embracing our frailty—our humanness. We literally cry out for help, recognizing our inability to take care of ourselves. As we get older, though, we lose this ability. We put our heads down and come to believe we are self-sustaining. Of course, in many senses, this is a good thing. As adults, we do need to provide for ourselves and care for others. But what we lose is the reality of our own frailty, the acknowledgment that we can and often must rely on others—and instead we believe that we are the end, that we are the gods of at least our own lives.

Instead of coming to grips with what seem to be unacceptable inadequacies, frailties, or weaknesses, we continue on in pretending to be more god than human, rejecting humanity. These stunning words from the poet-philosopher David Whyte perfectly describe the human condition:

> One of the interesting qualities of being human is, by the look of it, we're the only part of creation that can actually refuse to be ourselves. And as far as I can see, there's no other part of the world that can do that, you know? The cloud is the cloud; the mountain is the mountain; the tree is the tree; the hawk is the hawk. . . .
>
> But we, as human beings, are really quite extraordinary in that we can actually refuse to be ourselves. We can get afraid of the way we are. . . .
>
> So one of the astonishing qualities of being human is the measure of our reluctance to be here, actually. And I think one of the great necessities of self-knowledge is understanding and even tasting the single-malt essence of your own reluctance to be here.[7]

The truth is that we struggle with our human status. We don't like the lowly position of our actual lives, in which things happen outside of our control—injury, heartbreak, loss, aging, disappearance, and death. Richard Rohr calls it our basic resistance to life—this refusal "to accept what is, to accept ourselves, others, the past, our own mistakes, and the imperfection and idiosyncrasies of almost everything."[8] Our ways of thinking and acting reflect that we'd rather be God, at least over our lives, and our inability to be so causes sin, shame, anxiety, and fear.

To accept that we are human, then, is to accept that we do not sustain ourselves; we are not the center of the universe; we will make mistakes, fail, and disappoint; we do not have control over most things in even our own lives; our bodies will age and break down; and we will die. Isn't it interesting, then, that most self-help books on topics like temptation, shame, anxiety, and fear are about overcoming or conquering these things that are fundamental pieces of our humanness? What if they are not to be conquered but surrendered? Not given into but given over? Perhaps what's best for us is not to get over the shame, anxiety, and fear we carry but rather to draw near to these things and seek to encounter God within them. But in order to do that, we must look square in the face how we have developed crutches and coping practices around the parts of ourselves that we'd rather avoid.

COPING WITH OUR HUMANITY

Consider for a moment what you do with your body when you are afraid or anxious or ashamed. Perhaps you cross your arms across your chest and hold tight. Or you ball your hands into fists and tighten your shoulders. Maybe you curl up so your extremities feel close, put your hands over your face, or seek a solitary place that's small and confining.

We try to protect ourselves when we feel vulnerable to harm. And interestingly, we do this with our bodies even when the apparent harm is emotional or spiritual. We look around for a way to cover ourselves—as Adam and Eve did in the Garden—with the thought that we don't want to be hurt. In other words, we all have ways we seek to manage so-called negative emotions or painful memories and experiences. We all have ways of thinking to protect ourselves and ways of acting to numb ourselves, escape our actual reality, or attempt to control what we have no dominion over. The internal methods are psychological defense mechanisms—what psychologist Joseph Burgo calls "lies we tell ourselves to evade pain."[9] These defense mechanisms include *repression* (pushing certain thoughts or experienes away from our consciousness), *denial* (refusing to acknowledge something we know to be true), *displacement* (directing a feeling at someone other than its source), *reaction formation* (deeming a feeling or urge inappropriate), *splitting* (resolving ambiguity by creating two opposing ideas), *idealization* (elevating the ordinary or human to the status of perfection), *projection* (criticizing someone for doing something wrong when you are actually the responsible one), and *control* (adopting certain behaviors that give us a sense that we can control the uncontrollable).[10] These defense mechanisms assert themselves without our knowledge or consent, and often, those around us see them before we do. We don't decide to employ defense mechanisms; they are all *unconscious processes*[11]—processes that are "etched" into "the neural connections and pathways in the brain" over time.[12] The good news is, we actually can develop new, healthier pathways over time. We'll always battle the old pathways, though. As Joseph Burgo notes, "they've been around much longer, with years of heavy traffic to dig them deeper."[13]

These actions that arise out of our psychological defense mechanisms are what we often call coping practices. Some of our coping practices are destructive in and of themselves and some are relatively benign, but all of them have the potential to inhibit our relationships and health. And for anyone seeking to live a deeply satisfying life, this is a problem. But even more critically, for those of us who seek to participate with Christ in the world, to join his work of redemption, these coping practices are even more problematic. They hinder our ability to encounter and experience God's presence, to allow ourselves to be enlivened and transformed by the Holy Spirit, and to live the life Jesus came to the world to give us. Think of my plane routine. I distract and numb myself for the entire flight so that my mind and body have no opportunity to notice they are afraid. While I block out fear, I also close the doors to God. I have no room to encounter him under those circumstances.

I don't know if you've got your own ways of numbing,

escaping, or controlling when you're feeling anxiety, fear, or shame or acting out of brokenness or sin. My guess is that you do (if not, please call me immediately to share your secret). The good news is that God is familiar and patient with this arena of human struggle. Think of Jesus' agony in the garden of Gethsemane. What he wanted most as a human man was to escape his coming crucifixion and death. He prayed three times that God would accomplish his work in some other way and take away the suffering he would face (Matthew 26:39-44). Though Jesus knew his suffering would end in him returning to eternal communion with the Father, his human mind struggled not to numb, escape, or control. But, showing us how to be dependent on and surrendered to God in his weakness (that is, truly human), he stayed present and turned himself over to God. He knew that even the suffering and death he would endure would not be as bad as an encounter and communion with God would be good. God knows firsthand our human struggle to be dependent on him.

In fact, God's Word shows us many facets of our inclination toward coping with our humanity. In Luke 10, we read about Martha, who knew well how to distract herself and distance herself from the present:

> As Jesus and his disciples were on their way, he
> came to a village where a woman named Martha
> opened her home to him. She had a sister called

Mary, who sat at the Lord's feet listening to what he said. But Martha was distracted by all the preparations that had to be made. She came to him and asked, "Lord, don't you care that my sister has left me to do the work by myself? Tell her to help me!"

"Martha, Martha," the Lord answered, "you are worried and upset about many things, but few things are needed—or indeed only one. Mary has chosen what is better, and it will not be taken away from her."

LUKE 10:38-42, NIV

We aren't told all that Martha was feeling that drives her to be so worried about the dinner she's preparing, but we know she resented that Mary had left her to do the meal preparation herself. Notice—Jesus doesn't say anything until Martha expresses her anger and resentment toward Mary (and toward Jesus for not correcting Mary's behavior). He doesn't force his way in; he waits for her to ask for help. Why didn't she feel comfortable sitting at the feet of Jesus, as Mary did? Why did she have to busy herself to the point of total distraction? Maybe Mary had a habit of letting Martha do all the work in their family and Martha thought she finally had someone who'd be on her side. Maybe Martha aimed for perfection in what she made for fear that Jesus would judge her worth based on her results. Maybe she was worried about what she might find in herself once she stopped and allowed herself to be seen apart from her work. Jesus says she is "worried and upset about many things" (Luke 10:41, NIV).

Whatever the cause, we can relate to allowing our own busyness to act as a barrier between us and a potential encounter with Jesus. We have many of the same insecurities and worries Martha had. What we see from this story is that Jesus deemed it better for Martha to be with him than any other options. But he is so gentle with her: "My dear Martha," he says (NLT). He doesn't shame her or attempt to diminish her. He speaks truth to her because he wants what's best for her. But he does this with great love.

Wanting to offer Jesus warm and inviting hospitality isn't a sin. But more is going on here. We see it in Martha's request for help, and we see it in Jesus' response. Martha allowed her shame, fear, anxiety, or brokenness to leak out. We don't know what psychological defense mechanisms kick in, but we know something is happening because she's engaged in a coping practice: busyness. By staying busy, Martha can cover whatever pain or discomfort she is feeling and take pride in her helpfulness as compared to her sister Mary.

But as good as it might make her feel to demonstrate how service-oriented she is (especially toward Jesus!), she is missing out. She isn't leaving room. Consider yourself in her position. Jesus—your Lord and Savior, the King of kings, God in the flesh, and the one who sees all that is in you and loves you unendingly—is sitting on your couch.

Instead of sitting with him in awe and reverence to bask in his love and grace, you decide to go into the other room to cut up cheese and arrange the crackers just so on your best platter. Hopefully, this strikes you as both ridiculous and something you might just do. After all, we do this all the time. Our experiences aren't necessarily as obvious as Martha's because Jesus isn't physically present with us. When we are drowning in our woundedness and broken-ness, though, do we consider that Jesus *is* present, waiting for us to invite him in? Are we capable or even willing to put down our defenses and see what might happen?

In one of Jesus' parables in the book of Luke, we learn of a rich man who may also strike us as relatable (which was Jesus' intent; Luke 12:16-21). He has a fertile farm. As he begins to accumulate more and more, he decides to build bigger barns to store up all that his land has pro-duced. As he builds, he envisions his future—a time when he has stored up enough, whatever "enough" may be—sitting back with his feet up, eating, drinking, and being merry for the rest of his life. He has no worries and feels completely secure.

It's hard not to read the first part of this story (as if we don't know the end) and think, *That seems pretty wise. Save up and retire. Not bad.* But God calls this man a fool. Not because saving is foolish—but because this man found his security and placed his trust in his stuff and his own abili-ties instead of in God. His vision of himself kicking back demonstrates his desire to be king, master of his own life.

In his accumulation of wealth, he left no room for relationship with God (Luke 12:21).

Jesus told this parable to warn against distracting and numbing ourselves with possessions. It's hard to imagine a more apt story for our day of consumerism and wealth accumulation. Jesus told his listeners, "Life is not measured by how much you own" (Luke 12:15). Most people would acknowledge the truth of this. And yet, if we look around our houses and neighborhoods, we don't live like we believe it. We buy all kinds of things that we don't need, and even rent property (storage lockers) in which to keep it all. (When my daughter was little, she suggested that maybe homeless people could live in the storage lockers we had all over the suburbs of Chicago. It made more sense to her that we would house people rather than stuff we didn't need.) What is this about?

If we examine the moments we click the "buy now" button on whatever website we've discovered or stick our credit card into the payment machine at any of the hundreds of stores designed to promise us satisfaction, we may discover our motivations. Often, we are coping—avoiding, distracting, numbing. We are anxious or fearful about something, and we're trying to distract ourselves to avoid those feelings. Or we are numbing shame or seeking to satisfy nameless longings. Online shopping has made these tendencies even more profound. We continue, in our modern day, to store up stuff and find our security in it, forgetting and dismissing that God is even reaching out to us.

Underlying these desires to cope, we can usually find our own brokenness, shame, anxiety, or fear. Indeed, as Brené Brown points out, "the most powerful need for numbing seems to come from combinations of . . . shame, anxiety, and disconnection."[14] We cannot or do not want to face the cracked pieces of our humanity, so we cope.

IDENTIFYING OUR COPING PRACTICES

Coping practices are about as varied as we are. But there are some common ones: overindulging in alcohol, using drugs to escape or numb, binge-watching Netflix shows, mindlessly scrolling through social media, zoning out, engaging in pornography or other sexual conduct absent of intimacy and love, overeating, impulsive shopping or over-spending, overexercising, compulsive gambling, and cutting. We know these are coping practices because they are ways of escaping or numbing us out of the moment—and they don't ultimately meet the desire we are seeking to sat-isfy. But the signs that we're tempted to cope aren't always so obvious. Perhaps we bite our nails or fingers, pick at our lips, crack our knuckles, or bounce our leg. Something is upsetting us, and these small physical signs may soon give way to more intense coping practices.

Perhaps you are very aware of your coping practices and can easily name them without any effort. Maybe you just know when you feel off and you are leaking, but you're not sure yet the ways you seek to cope. In the end, there's no real magic to identifying the ways you cope. It's a matter of paying attention and asking others who love you and whose opinions you trust. The people you interact with most will have insight you might not be able to access otherwise.[15]

Brené Brown poses a great question that gets at identifying coping practices: "Are my choices comforting and nourishing my spirit, or are they temporary reprieves from vulnerability and difficult emotions ultimately diminishing my spirit? Are my choices leading to my Wholeheartedness, or do they leave me feeling empty and searching?"[16] Her phrasing here is important: It puts the focus on what nourishes or drains us as individuals. That is, *my* unhealthy ways of coping with painful emotions may not be unhealthy for you, and vice versa.

Don't be afraid of taking a close look at how you cope. I'm right there with you. As I've been working through my own ways of coping, I've noticed that sometimes I reach for my phone, hit my Facebook icon, and start scrolling. I do this at times when I am simply bored. But other times, I do it when I'm with others—and it must seem very rude—which makes me wonder what I'm trying to escape in those moments. We're all a work in progress. May God guide us in every way.

REFLECTION QUESTIONS

Before you begin, note that wrestling through this can bring up shame (ironic, I know). Ask God to help you stay above this shame and fill you with his presence. These questions are not intended to induce shame but to spark awareness that will lead you into deeper communion with God. If you do begin to sense shame rising within you, identify it, and include it in your journaling. If it becomes too overwhelming or dominant, take a break.

1. For the next couple of weeks, keep a record of when you do things that you think could be ways of coping with feelings you'd rather not experience. At the end of that period, look back and see what sticks out to you.

2. What happens after you have an argument with your spouse or a family member? Where do you go? What do you do? How long does it take for you to feel okay again?

3. When you are alone or feeling lonely, what do you do?

4. Do you have any "precoping practice" habits (biting your nails, etc.) that might lead to more insight about your coping practices?

5. Are you able to identify an underlying cause of your coping practice(s)? Do you notice a susceptibility to a particular sin or unhealthy behavior? Shame? Anxiety? Fear?

6. What role does God have in your heart and mind as you employ coping practices?

PART II

PRACTICING GOD'S PRESENCE

The negative and life-diminishing ways we manage our brokenness and uncomfortable emotions are physical—things we do with our bodies in hopes of making our minds and hearts feel better. We can tell that these coping practices are unhealthy because they never lead us into true nourishment and life—which, ultimately, is trust in and dependence on God. But here's the good news: Our bodies also offer restorative and healthy paths to actually entering into God's presence more fully and opening us to his healing and transformation. And if we look at Scripture, we can find the amazing reality that this is God's desire and design for us.

For the last four years, I have been studying the apostle Paul's letter to the churches in Rome, and Paul's words in Romans 12:1-3 are never far from my mind. They have been there when I wake up, in moments of impatience, sadness, anxiety, shame, and fear. They have come up as I've pondered divisive comments I see on social media, and even most recently, as I reflect on the worldwide pandemic caused by COVID-19. In these three verses, Paul is telling us something critical about the role of our bodies and our ability to encounter God and be transformed. I know it's tempting to skip over block quotes, but try reading this passage slowly and see if there's anything specific you notice:

> I urge you, brothers and sisters, in view of God's mercy, to offer your bodies as a living sacrifice, holy and pleasing to God—this is your true and proper worship. Do not conform to the pattern of this world, but be transformed by the renewing of your mind. Then you will be able to test and approve what God's will is—his good, pleasing and perfect will. . . .
>
> Do not think of yourself more highly than you ought, but rather think of yourself with sober judgment, in accordance with the faith God has distributed to each of you.
>
> ROMANS 12:1-3, NIV

So much meaning, instruction, and depth! Certainly I would have wanted whomever was reading this letter aloud the first time (probably Phoebe; Romans 16:1) to go back and read these words again and again. After all, Paul is speaking to *Christians* in this letter. They have already made that first decision to follow Jesus. They had likely left generational traditions and beliefs and were putting themselves at risk as Christians in Rome. And they had assented to certain truths about Jesus. Knowing all they had already sacrificed, though, Paul instructs them to offer even more. The word *body* (Greek, *sōma*) is not limited in the ways we might think today. It is intended to include the "entire person in all its created vibrancy and aliveness."[1] Paul is urging Christians to turn over their whole selves, holding nothing back.

But we must also assume he uses *bodies* for a specific purpose: acknowledging that after deciding to follow Jesus, humans don't become disembodied, spiritual beings. Humans must deal with the fact that, as theologian N. T. Wright says, they live "within the world of space, time, and matter" and "within the multiple pressures and temptations that this places upon us."[2] To be a follower of Jesus is not about merely holding a set of beliefs but allowing those beliefs to shape entirely what our bodies do. Our faith, as our lives, is to be embodied.[3]

Paul goes further with this point, instructing us not to "conform to the pattern of the world." The "pattern of the world" during Paul's day meant the way of the Roman

Empire. New Testament scholar Scot McKnight describes what this would have been:

> embattled competition for honor and status
> and glory, of idolatries formed in the dust of
> suppressing knowledge of God as Creator, of
> sexual indulgence outside the Creator's norms,
> of rebellion against Roman authorities, and most
> especially of any life that is not determined by
> love.[4]

This is no different than the way of our world in the twenty-first century, at least in the West. And God calls us today, as he called first-century Christians, to live differently from the rest of the world. Followers of Jesus should look different not just because of what we believe but because *what we believe dictates what we do with our bodies on a daily basis.* This is no easy endeavor, of course. Indeed, Paul began this part of his letter by telling the Roman Christians that to live this way would be a sacrifice that they'd have to choose to offer. So it is for us. We will find ourselves struggling not to allow ourselves to get caught in the pattern of the world—its ways of thinking, approach to others, views of sexuality, values and primary concerns, and ways of acting in times of plenty and in times of hardship. When we employ our coping practices, isn't this precisely what we're giving in to? The patterns of the world?

So how do we remain open to God, even in the midst

of our own brokenness, shame, anxiety, and fear? How do we resist what the world tells us will help? Listen to the last of Paul's words in this passage: "Do not think of yourself more highly than you ought, but rather think of yourself with sober judgment, in accordance with the faith God has distributed to each of you." Paul is reminding his listeners first that they are human, living in limited, created, and sustained-by-God bodies, and that they are no more valuable than their fellow humans, who are limited and sustained in the same ways.

Paul is saying something else here as well. When he speaks of "the faith God has distributed to each of you," he does not mean the amount of faith a person has. Rather, he's referring to the spiritual gift each particular person has been assigned within the larger "body"—the church.[5] The "how" of opening to God's presence begins with humility—as Scot McKnight puts it, "seeing oneself through God's assignment for one in the Body of Christ" and acting in that role.[6] Humility is a posture of the mind and of the body. Thinking you are open isn't quite enough; the body must be involved.

This is why just after Paul tells us to offer our bodies as a living sacrifice, he spends pages listing out various ways of behaving: living in harmony with one another, honoring others above yourself, working hard, rejoicing, being patient, helping those in need, and practicing hospitality, among many others. But these lists are not, as is often thought, to be taken as tasks Christians are to do. Rather, these are *ways of being* that open us to God's presence and transformative work.

Let's consider, then, what this means for our places of brokenness, shame, anxiety, and fear. Negative coping mechanisms cause us to avoid God's transforming work. But these things Paul is talking about—these positions of the mind and body that open us to what God wants to do—what if they're the pathway to healing the most vulnerable parts of our souls?

I don't know about you, but these ways of being Paul is talking about aren't what I would have thought of first in my desire to encounter God. And I certainly wouldn't have thought they'd increase my chances of finding healing in the wounded parts of myself. What Paul is talking about seems too, I don't know, external and others-oriented to meaningfully address something so internal and personal. I have long thought of opening to God as a matter of will, a decision that I make in my quiet space alone at home. I have presented myself to God in prayer and, with my words, surrendered my whole self—body, mind, and soul. I have meant it sincerely. I have deeply longed for God to change whatever needed to be changed, to take whatever he wanted to take.

But it turns out that surrender doesn't happen by internal decision alone, absent the participation of the physical body in the church body. Sure, in the face of fear, I can yell, "I'm not afraid anymore!" like Kevin McAllister did at the furnace in *Home Alone*. I can say, "I trust God completely" (and mean it). But encountering God requires more than mental assent. Or, put differently, in order to truly open spiritually, we need to engage with the world physically.

That's where we're going in Part II—into the tangible, into the ways we can engage our bodies so that we can open ourselves to encountering God. We're going to explore six practices drawn out of Romans 12, ways of being that give life and help us walk through our brokenness, shame, anxiety, and fear with our eyes open to God's transforming work. Each chapter explains a particular practice and offers some ideas of how to put that practice to use. The key to these practices is moving with body, mind, and heart into God's presence and making room for the healing Jesus Christ provides.

As we engage our bodies in these ways, inviting God into these movements, I suspect something is going to happen to us. We are going to become more vulnerable—open to the possibility of harm—in order for God to heal and mend and transform us. It's not going to be safe. And it's not going to be predictable. I cannot know how you will encounter God and what specifically God will do in you (or in me, for that matter). But what I do know is that as we turn away from our coping practices and toward the life-giving paths God offers us, our hearts will become increasingly surrendered, humble, free, grounded, generous, and connected. We are going to be less broken, ashamed, anxious, and afraid. Together, we are going to have to trust the Holy Spirit's work in this. Whatever does happen (whether we notice it immediately or down the road) will be better than any substitute we might be tempted to try.

As Paul might say: "Who will free us from these lives marked by brokenness, shame, anxiety, and fear? Thank God! The answer is in Jesus Christ our Lord. Amen!"[7]

CHAPTER 3

SURRENDER YOUR BODY

But I trust in you, LORD;
I say, "You are my God."
My times are in your hands;
deliver me from the hands of my enemies,
from those who pursue me.

PSALM 31:14-15, NIV

When I was twelve or so, I flew from Chicago to Houston with my grandma and sister. I was excited because this was my first time flying—everything was new. The smell of jet fuel; all the restaurants and shops and people at the airport; the long tube you had to walk through to board; the flight attendants and pilots welcoming you aboard; the gifts inside the seat-back pocket; the tiny cups of 7UP and bags of peanuts; the amazing freedom of taking off and then seeming to float in the sky and looking down at the earth, everything in miniature from way up in the clouds. I don't have an actual memory of this, but I suspect that on this very first flight, my body was relaxed and my arms and hands were busy with a "search and find" puzzle or a book.

At some point during the flight, we hit an air pocket. The plane suddenly dropped for what felt like an eternity before recovering. I heard gasps and yelps, not quite screams, and felt my stomach drop out of my body. I don't remember anything after that except that we ended up in Houston as planned, landing smoothly and safely. And since that time, I've been unable to be free of fear when I fly. About two weeks before I'm scheduled to fly somewhere, I begin to have stress dreams, feel anxious during the day for no discernible reason, and am short-tempered. Anticipatory fear strangles the life out of up to fourteen days before I fly. As the departure day gets closer, I fantasize of ways to get out of the trip, even if it's a vacation I long for and am excited about. When I board the plane, my insides shake and my palms sweat. By the time I get to my seat, I don't care about the gifts in the seat back (there are few these days, anyway) or the tiny cups of 7UP and peanuts (it's pretzels now). No, I am fully engaged in trying to convince myself that I can endure anything for whatever the number of hours this flight will be—two, four, sixteen. And while my mind seems to buy this con job, my body will have no part of it. My breathing starts to quicken, I feel unable to get air past my throat and into my lungs, and my legs can't be kept still. I cross my arms for most of the flight, as if my body will fall apart otherwise.

It's been over thirty years now that I have struggled with this at-times-overwhelming fear. I haven't ever actually cancelled a trip or gotten off a flight because of it, but I have considered both seriously. During the years when I flew two or three times a week for my work, the fear lessened as I grew used to the movements of the plane. But give me a couple months between flights, and I'm back where I started.

I can't seem to overcome this fear. I even took flying lessons so I could understand the way planes work. I learned how sturdy they are, what turbulence is, and all the checks a pilot must conduct before getting off the ground. I've talked to pilots extensively to learn from them what makes them nervous (almost nothing, as it turns out). I've researched why air pockets exist and what could happen if a plane hits them. I check the weather religiously for weeks leading up to a flight, praying that winds will be low and the skies will be clear. In other words, I gather information, thinking that perhaps knowing more will make me less afraid.

During a flight, I have to medicate myself and trick my mind into believing I am safe. I have a cocktail of substances I take—a pill for anxiety (on top of my regular anxiety medicine), and if it's a flight over six hours, a melatonin for sleep. I also listen to worship songs that I have a long history with, so they feel like friends. If those coping practices "don't work," I watch a favorite television show on my iPad and try to trick myself into thinking I'm home on the couch.

As I write this, I can feel my body tighten. It's wondering if we are going to fly soon. I also feel shame. Haven't I heard the statistics about it being more likely that I'll die in a car accident than going down in a plane? Don't I know plane travel is safe? Yes, yes, I do know. My fear isn't reasonable. But it's still there and still powerful.

So what are all my coping practices, all my attempts to rationalize my way out of my fear, really about? I think, in the end, my fear of flying represents a much bigger issue: a lack of trust and surrender. Somewhere deep within, I do not feel safe, and I believe that preserving my life is the most important task I have.

We all respond and act in ways that reflect a lack of trust. As I write, we're months into the COVID-19 pandemic of 2020. The entire globe faces a dangerous and highly infectious virus, and there are wise steps to take in response. I myself stayed at home for months and rarely went out, wearing a face mask when I did. But the all-out panic and fear—and their destructive companions, anger and distrust—that have overtaken us as humans has been striking. I don't mean to judge whether our fears are justified, but I've been reflecting on how this pandemic has highlighted how afraid we are. The preservation of our lives, physically and materially, supersedes almost all else. Say, for example, we have the opportunity to serve and love another person and to encounter God in that interaction . . . but we knew we'd be at risk of exposure to the virus. We would probably choose not to expose ourselves, right?

Perhaps another fear comes to mind as you consider where you lack trust, and maybe you cope in a very different way. Fear, sin, shame, and anxiety all can be signs that we're grasping for control where control belongs to God alone. The question, then, is this: If we cannot think our way into control or surrender, what else can we do to turn our trust over to God and surrender our illusion of control?

THE CALL TO SURRENDER

God does not force us to trust him. He gives each one of us the ability to ignore and dismiss him, even as he sustains our every breath. This independence suits us just fine much of the time, particularly when things are going well for us. But as we lean further and further into our autonomy, we forget God and allow ourselves (perhaps unknowingly) to be shaped by the world around us.

In a sense, Scripture warns against this independence from beginning to end. Indeed, we see God making a singular plea to humanity throughout history: *surrender to my love and care.* Sometimes the plea comes in the form of God reminding humans that he is God (and that, accordingly, they are not; Exodus 6:29; Isaiah 41:10; 45:5). Sometimes his plea comes in allowing his people to exercise their autonomy so they will discover the disastrous results (think Genesis 3, when Adam and Eve ate from the tree, or 1 Samuel 8, when the Israelites ask for a king so they can be like the other nations). But in Jesus, we see both the exemplar of a person surrendered to God the Father and a tangible reminder of what God asks of us. Jesus made the same plea that God has been making throughout history:

> If any of you wants to be my follower, you must give up your own way, take up your cross, and follow me. If you try to hang on to your life, you will lose it. But if you give up your life for my sake and for the sake of the Good News, you will save it. And what do you benefit if you gain the whole world but lose your own soul? Is anything worth more than your soul?
>
> MARK 8:34-37

Anyone could teach such things, of course. There is nothing sacrificial about telling others to take up their cross to follow you. There's nothing difficult in asking someone else to lose their life for you. But Jesus never asked his followers to do something that he himself would not do. The very fact that he came into the world, purposely limiting himself and subjecting himself to pain and death by becoming human (Philippians 2:8), is hard to fathom. But also, Jesus gave his life willingly—not for his own sake but for the sake of the world: "No one takes [my life] from me, but I lay it down of my own accord" (John 10:18, NIV). In his most agonizing moment of life, Jesus surrendered himself to the will of his Father: "'*Abba*, Father,' he said, 'everything is possible for you. Take this cup from me. Yet not what I will, but what you will'" (Mark 14:36, NIV). At the very end, as he hangs on the cross, his body naked and splayed in the most vulnerable of ways, we are told of no battle for survival, but rather Jesus' words: "Father, into your hands I commit my spirit" (Luke 23:46, NIV).

When I first became a Christian, I wanted to follow Jesus with everything I was—to turn from my selfish ways, take up my cross, and follow him. And as best I knew how, I released my life to Jesus. Many of us can look back and identify seasons in which we are sure we did the same.

Yet . . . we will never reach the end of surrender. Each of us has ways of thinking, habits, and heart conditions that we hold on to with a tight grip. Holding on so hard to an illusion of control leads us right back to the place of despair. Whether we realize it or not, we continually respond to God's invitation to further surrender with resistance, wanting instead to exercise sovereignty over our own lives. We cross our arms, ball our hands into fists, and distract ourselves.

Undoubtedly these responses are driven at least in part by rebellion and sin. But for those who have gotten to the end of themselves or long to surrender to God, could it be that there's something else? Perhaps we also need a little help in knowing *how* to surrender to God's love and care. Surrender sounds like a worthy goal, but I get a little stuck on what exactly it means in my day-to-day life. How do I actually do it? What does it mean to hang on to my life versus giving it up? And assuming I know the answer to this question, how do I actually do that? I continually get in my own way; perhaps you can relate.

Surrender is a struggle because our culture forms us into tightfisted self-seekers. Not to mention, over the last thousand or more years, parts of the church have reduced salvation to the forgiveness of sins alone, which requires nothing more than mental assent and offers very little advice as to the role of our bodies or what to do in our everyday, bodily lives.[1] Indeed, dozens of generations have dismissed and denigrated Paul's call to an embodied faith.[2] But if we want to meet God in the midst of our fear, brokenness, shame, and anxiety, we must be willing to learn how to surrender.

Let's start by talking about what surrender means. Most of us can conjure images of troops waving a white flag in war time, a victim raising her hands in the face of a bank robber, a child yelling "uncle" when an older sibling twists their arm behind their back, or a person giving in to a particularly strong temptation. We associate surrender with a weak position in which we are forced to give in to a stronger person or face death, pain, or some other kind of discomfort. No wonder we don't like the idea of surrendering.

But what if we could come to understand surrender differently? What if we could see surrender as releasing effort, tension, and fear to someone we trust?[3] David Benner paints a picture of surrender as a kind of floating: "Floating is putting your full weight on the water trusting that you will be supported. It is letting go of your natural instincts to fight against sinking. Only then do you discover that you are supported."[4] Surrender is one of those things we recognize best when it's missing.

Not long ago, my husband got me a gift certificate for an hour in a float tank. This relaxation technique, in which you get into a personal pool filled with ten inches of water and 1,000 pounds of epsom salts, is supposed to boost your immune system, help with muscle pain, and calm your mind (among other things). All I had to do was lay on my back in the water and close my eyes. Sounds pretty simple, right? Well, not so much. If I didn't know I had anxiety before this "relaxation exercise," I would have known by five minutes in. I could not trust that I would float. Although I assumed the proper position, I held on to the side so I could remain in control. And as soon as I would start to relax, and realize it, I would jerk with fear, open my eyes, and be bombarded by worried thoughts all over again. I was like Peter walking on water, feeling his trust slip away and the waves creep higher. I couldn't think my way into relaxing. As much as my mind wanted to, my body still had the most sway. My body—seemingly apart from my own mind—decides when it is safe and when it is not.

Our bodies remember, in a way that goes beyond pure memory, when we have felt unsafe and remind us when they feel unsafe again. That's why surrender cannot be a mental exercise alone—our bodies must be given over, too; they must be integrated into our spiritual life.[5] But they, too, must feel safe in order to relax and trust.[6]

The place I floated has since gone out of business—not because anyone sank, but I do wonder if it was because not enough people were willing to surrender. As Richard Rohr says, surrender of any kind—whether privilege, body, will, or life—"always feels like dying."[7] And yet, as C. S. Lewis reminds us, this kind of surrender "is far easier than what we are all trying to do instead."[8]

Surrender is a relatively easy concept to understand when we're talking about literal floating. If you've been in a pool or body of water, you know what it feels like to float or not to float, how you're able to release your body or not in those circumstances. But what does the body have to do with surrendering our ego, our will, and our desires to God's care? Not to mention our brokenness, fear, anxiety, and shame?

Dallas Willard asserts that "our body is a primary *resource* for the spiritual life."[9] And, the apostle Paul tells us, it is through our bodies that we are to "honor God" (1 Corinthians 6:20, NIV). If we look at Romans 12–16, we see that bodies are a central part of lived transformation, an actively sacrificial part of our life with God. As we use our bodies as they're intended—to serve and honor God and others (rather than using them to serve our own needs and ambitions)—we will see our ego, will, and desires begin to bend toward loving others instead of self. Conversely, the less we do for others, the less we desire to do for others. Our bodily life, our lived-out experience, leads our spiritual life. Thus surrender in our bodily life leads to surrender in our spiritual life.

What does bodily surrender look like? In its most basic form, it's being fully present where we actually are (instead of worrying about the future or regretting the past). This may look like me allowing my body to relax in an airplane seat 35,000 feet above the ground. Or it may look like physically showing up for and being present to someone else. When I consider the essence of bodily surrender, I think of a time my daughter was sick as a young child. She didn't get the stomach flu often, but on this particular occasion, I sat with her on the cold tile of the bathroom floor as she leaned over the toilet. I rubbed her back and assured her she'd be okay. She shook and cried and was afraid. It was the middle of the night, and I was tired. The hard floor hurt my ankles, and the longer I sat there, the more my back stiffened. The smell sickened me. The night was not going as I had planned. But then something came over me (I wish I could say I prayed), and I realized how selfish I was being. I wasn't the sick one. I was merely inconvenienced. I exhaled, adjusted my body, and leaned in. As much as I tried to reassure my daughter with words, what she needed most was my presence. And it was a sacrifice for me to be there on the floor with her. At some point as she started to feel better, she said, "Thanks for sitting with me, Mom." My heart melted. All these years later, I still remember that moment.

Richard Rohr says surrender happens "when I let go of my judgments, my agenda, my tyrannical emotive life, my attachment to my positive or negative self-image."[10]

Yes. But more often than not, we try to do these things Rohr mentions as a mental exercise. If our bodies aren't involved, mental surrender rarely works. We will find ourselves returning again and again to our own judgments, agendas, emotions, and desired image. Our brokenness, shame, anxiety, and fear will distract and push us toward the escape or control we seek in our coping practices.[11] When we are physically present with other people, submitting to them in love and participating in their emotions, we can begin to get outside of ourselves and let go of these tyrants.

Now, please know that like anything in life, this tangible surrender takes practice. None of us will ever get to the level of perfection where practice is no longer needed. It's a lifelong endeavor. But as we practice bodily surrender, we will see God enter our lives and our brokenness in ways we never expected.

PRACTICE GUIDE

Many of us are disconnected from or dissatisfied with our bodies. Some of us are at all-out war with our bodies. Others of us have become consumed by our bodies and how they look or feel. We shouldn't be surprised by this. Much of our brokenness is expressed through our bodies: Our shame is often a result of what our bodies look like and how they have been abused or used in the past; our anxiety frequently relates to how our bodies look or respond (or fail to respond) in different situations or how they might be hurt; and our fear traces back to a lack of control over what happens to our bodies—aging, illness, disease, and death. But as we enter into this journey of facing our areas of brokenness and asking God to transform them, we can engage in three practices each day to begin to surrender our bodies to his love and care.

First, because humility underpins surrender, we should start there, with a body posture practice that reminds us of our lowly, creaturely state and all but requires us not to think of ourselves more highly than we ought. As we are able to see our bodies as wholly sustained by God and subject to God, we are more able to entrust ourselves to his care. In a position of trust, we open ourselves to God's presence, and when we are threatened by our own brokenness, shame, anxiety, and fear, we are more likely to experience peace and engage our bodies in healthy ways. This is what I'd ask you to try, though it may feel awkward or silly at first, and see how God might meet you.

Surrender Your Body

- Choose some quiet instrumental music that will help you relax your mind and heart.

- Lay flat on your back on the floor, with your arms and legs spread in a position of vulnerability.

- Notice the ways in which you feel exposed and vulnerable; notice where your body hurts or feels uncomfortable;

notice your breath as it comes and goes without your attention or intention; notice your heartbeat as it keeps rhythm without your attention or intention. Allow yourself to be sobered by the inability you have to continue your breath or sustain your heartbeat.

· Inventory the parts of your body aloud, acknowledging God's role in making and sustaining those parts and offering each part as a gift to be used for God's glory. If a particular part of your body has been a tool in your brokenness, shame, anxiety, or fear, name that aloud. Here's a personal example:

Loving God, here I am. I am so vulnerable and small in your presence. You sustain my every breath and every heartbeat. Here are my feet. They have caused great shame for me because they sweat in the heat, and I can't wear flip-flops without feeling embarrassed and ugly. And yet these are the feet I have. I offer them to you to take me where you lead, to allow me to stand when you call, and to serve you and others. Here are my legs. They have been strong and yet they grow weak and wider as I age. They run slower, jump lower. I offer them to you. Here are my sexual organs and reproductive parts. I have experienced pleasure and pain in these parts. I offer them to you. Help me to honor you with these parts of my body. . . .

You can continue from there, offering each part. Doing this practice each day (or at least a couple times a week) can be an offering. It is a sacrifice, this opening of yourself—each part of your body—to God's loving presence and to his transformation. It is an expression of holy vulnerability. You don't necessarily need to go through each body part each time, but do it regularly enough that you don't retake control over those parts but continue to surrender them. And remember—this practice ends up being little more than lying on the floor unless you use your body for God's purposes and to serve others out of it.

Surrender Yourself

Another practice of surrender involves the actual turning over of ourselves—our bodies, yes, but also our self-image, ego, plans, control, attachments, loved ones, agenda, emotions. And our broken parts—shame, anxiety, and fear. All of it. All of us. This practice seeks to have the body do what the mind and heart desire—to let go and turn over to God's love and care. In this process, we seek to express an inward desire by outward action, something that has a long history in our faith.

- Close your hands in fists. As you grip them tightly, consider what your mind and heart are holding on to in a similar way. Maybe you're clinging to several different things—your expectations about how your work life was going to go; the relationship you thought you'd have with your son, but you don't; the shame about the pounds you've gained in the last couple of years. Notice the emotions you feel around whatever has arisen. Allow the ways you've tried to cope with these anxieties or disappointments or sins or missed expectations to come to mind. Your hands should be getting fatigued, tired of being held so tightly. This is the tiredness that your soul feels—tired of holding on and longing for a release.

- Now, open your hands and allow your palms to face the floor. If you're afraid to just drop everything, then squat down and place all that you've held on the ground. Let your relaxed hands speak your release of each thing you held so tightly. For example, "Father, I give you this anxiety about flying. I'm so tired of holding it. I'm letting it go and placing myself in your care." This practice of release is something we'll need to do often, especially if we pick everything we've dropped back up again.

- Lastly, turn your hands over, palms up, in a posture of receiving, and receive into them these words of Jesus: "Come to me, all of you who are weary and carry heavy burdens, and I will give you rest. Take my yoke upon you. Let me teach you, because I am humble and gentle at heart, and you will find rest for your souls. For my yoke is easy to bear, and the burden I give you is light" (Matthew 11:28-30).

This practice is easier to do in semipublic places, like at your desk at work or standing in line at the grocery store. You can do it multiple times a day as you feel your shoulders tighten or your brow furrow. I've found it humbling to recognize how often I'm holding tightly to my own ways, refusing to release and surrender.

> I pray that God, the source of hope, will fill you completely with joy and peace because you trust in him. Then you will overflow with confident hope through the power of the Holy Spirit.
>
> ROMANS 15:13

REFLECTION QUESTIONS

1. When you think of surrendering your life, or giving up your life for the sake of Christ and the Good News, what image comes to mind? What does surrender look like?

2. What are some ways you have tried to surrender in the past—but haven't been able to? What has worked? How do you know?

3. How attuned would you say you are to your body and the ways it speaks to you about your level of stress and surrender? How do you know?

4. What brokenness, shame, anxiety, or fear have you tried to think your way out of? What exactly did you do? How did it work?

5. What would you like God to help you surrender to his love and care? What concerns do you have about turning that over to him?

CHAPTER 4

PRAY COMMON PRAYERS

Lord God, almighty and everlasting Father, you have
brought us in safety to this new day: Preserve us with your
mighty power, that we may not fall into sin, nor be overcome
by adversity; and in all we do, direct us to the fulfilling
of your purpose; through Jesus Christ our Lord. Amen.

"COLLECT FOR GRACE," BOOK OF COMMON PRAYER

A number of years ago when I had a wisdom tooth
pulled, the oral surgeon gave me Vicodin to use if the pain
got too bad. So, in the evening when my head and mouth
ached, I took a pill with some water and laid back down on
the couch. Surely soon I'd be feeling better.

But that's not what happened. Not even fifteen minutes
later, I began to feel extremely nauseous. As I stumbled to
the bathroom, my head felt like it might explode, and my
whole body ached and shook. I coughed up everything in
my stomach and gasped for air. It took me a while to realize I was having a bad reaction to the Vicodin. I sat on the

floor and leaned against the cold toilet, tears leaking down my face. No one else was home. I was in agony. My phone was in the other room still, and I couldn't get up.

I tried to pray for help, that God would remove the pain and allow me to get back to the couch. But I couldn't even form the thoughts to make words. I wished I could call to mind someone else's words, that some cry to God was so ingrained in my mind that I didn't have to think through the pain. I longed to connect with God in this horrible moment.

But I hadn't ever taken the time to memorize any prayers; I had always relied on the fact that words would come with whatever need I had. Not this time. Psalm 23 was scrambled in my head—"Though I walk through the valley of death, your rod . . . What is the rest? Help me." The more I tried, the more jumbled the words became. I needed someone else there to pray for me. Or at least I needed someone else's words to use as my own.

At this point in my life, I hadn't given much thought to the role of the historical church in my relationship with God. I had considered the importance of the long-standing faithfulness of the church, the great writings of devotion and faith that have come out of the church, and even the connectivity that occurs across place and time when the church today reads Scripture and prayer out of the lectionary. Churches around the world share common prayers on Sunday mornings and share prayers together that Christians have been saying for a thousand or more years. This was moving to me, but it was little more than an interesting fact. I didn't actually feel connected to people around the world or Christians across the centuries.

But then I read a story about a former Catholic cardinal in Chicago, Joseph Bernardin. As a kid, I attended a school attached to one of the parishes Cardinal Bernardin presided over, and from time to time, he conducted mass there. His red-and-white robes and gentle face intrigued me. And although I knew little about him, there was something about the way he carried himself that I admired.

Cardinal Bernardin, of course, would have been the spiritual authority for many people, someone they would turn to for prayer, healing, confession, spiritual advice, and last rites. From all accounts, he was wise, discerning, and compassionate. He had a desire to see wrongs righted, and he cared for those who suffered. But despite this life of deep faith and devotion to God and others, Cardinal Bernardin lost his ability to pray toward the end of his life. He was dying of cancer, and his pain was so great that he could not concentrate long enough to pray. He wanted to and he tried, but bodily suffering overtook him. And so, when people came to visit him and asked what they could do for him, he asked that they would pray on his behalf.[1] He was asking them to bring him before the Lord. He needed someone else's words because he could no longer muster his own. Imagine the vulnerability and humility it took this man, so respected and honored for his prayer life, to admit that he needed someone else to carry him before Jesus.

Sickness, sadness, shame, or sin can shut us down and disable us from thinking clearly. And God always hears us; he knows our hearts and our wordless cries when we do not have words:

> The Holy Spirit helps us in our weakness. For example, we don't know what God wants us to pray for. But the Holy Spirit prays for us with groanings that cannot be expressed in words. And the Father who knows all hearts knows what the Spirit is saying, for the Spirit pleads for us believers in harmony with God's own will.
>
> ROMANS 8:26-27

In addition to this promise, we are offered another gift: When we are in deep pain or darkness, someone else's prayers or even faith can be a means of life support. This can look like a friend praying for us or our ability to borrow historical words and lean on historical faith in the moments or seasons in which we simply cannot draw on our own.

Think back to the story in Luke when a group of friends carried their paralyzed friend into the presence of Jesus so he could be healed (Luke 5:17-20). The man had no way of getting himself before Jesus. He couldn't walk; he likely had no way to get himself around other than to crawl or be carried. But unlike others we see in Gospel stories, this man had friends to help him. And from what we learn toward the end of the story, these were faith-filled friends. Indeed, we read that when Jesus saw the faith of *the friends*, he not only forgave the paralyzed man's sins but also healed his body so that he could walk. Nothing in the passage explicitly indicates that the paralyzed man had faith himself. Maybe he had lost all hope because of his physical ailments. But whatever his own faith looked like, he was permitted to borrow his friends' belief in Jesus' power to heal as his own.

Is this still a possibility today? When we are struggling to find words or even groans that bring ourselves before God in prayer, is it possible to rely on someone else's words?

WHAT IS COMMON PRAYER?

For many of us, spontaneous prayer is all we've really ever known. In fact, prayer is one of the most individualized, personal exercises we practice. We have emphasized the importance of going away by ourselves and praying to the Father, and we have, at least in the evangelical tradition, steered clear of any written, shared prayers for fear that such prayers reflect vain repetition or an impersonal, nominal faith.[2] We pray when we feel the need to pray, and the words we use are ours alone, a reflection of how we are feeling and what we need for ourselves or those we love. This kind of prayer is an invaluable practice to have and is critical to growing in intimacy with God.

Yet there are times we turn too far inward. Our prayers become self-centered and rote in their own way. We may lose focus and find ourselves thinking of something that happened at work or something we saw on social media. Even when we pray in church, we are often instructed or invited to close our eyes and find our own internal space separate from the bodies standing around us. We are praying, as Scot McKnight would say, *in the church* but not in this case *with the church*.[3] Individual prayers are particularly difficult when we are struggling with our brokenness, shame, anxiety, or fear—times when we tend to become isolated and self-focused, leading us to engage in our destructive coping practices, which, of course, lead to further isolation.

At the end of the day, we all face moments when spontaneous, individual prayer isn't enough—when words won't come, we have nothing to say, or we can't get past the idea that we feel like we're praying the same thing over and over. Or maybe there is a particular area of our lives that we simply can't be honest with ourselves about enough to pray. We might also have a hard heart or an ignorant heart about certain subjects or people. That's when we are invited into the richness of common prayer. Common prayer gives language and even faith to what we cannot.

Common prayers are historical prayers of the church (for example, the Psalms, the Lord's Prayer, or the prayers found in the Book of Common Prayer) as well as prayers that have been written by others which we can adapt as our own. In Judaism, Christianity, and Islam, common prayers began as a practice of fixed-hour prayer.[4] As we can see reflected in the

Psalms, the Jewish people had fixed times each day (morning, noon, and night) when they turned their attention to God to praise and pray (Psalm 55:17; 119:164; see also Daniel 6:10-11). During these set times, the Jewish people prayed the Psalms first and foremost. They chanted them together, they prayed them alone, and they memorized these prayers so that they became part of a common language. We see this as we review the many references and allusions Jesus made to the Psalms without having to cite his sources to those listening. The Psalms were largely internalized among the people. The Jewish people also recited the *Shema* in the morning and in the evening.[5] The *Shema* (a Hebrew word meaning "listen" or "hear"), which comes from the opening lines of the following verses, was first given to the Israelites by Moses.

> Listen, O Israel! The LORD is our God, the LORD
> alone. And you must love the LORD your God with
> all your heart, all your soul, and all your strength.
> And you must commit yourselves wholeheartedly
> to these commands that I am giving you today.
> Repeat them again and again to your children. Talk
> about them when you are at home and when you
> are on the road, when you are going to bed and
> when you are getting up.
> DEUTERONOMY 6:4-7

In the days of the early church, fixed-hour common prayers carried over into the lives of Christians. In fact, several of the events described in the book of Acts happened during these fixed-hour prayers. Peter and John healed a man on their way to the Temple for three-o'-clock prayer (Acts 3:1-8). When God gave Peter the vision on the rooftop that sparked Peter's realization that the gospel was for Gentiles too, Peter had gone up to pray for noon prayer (Acts 10:9-16).[6]

As history moved ahead, the church continued to pray both alone and in community, incorporating the Lord's Prayer along with the Psalms. The writings of the early church fathers reflect fixed-hour prayer as a regular practice of the second and third centuries, and by this time, the prayers had become "common" in the sense that "they employed the time-honored and time-polished prayers and recitations of the faith. Every Christian was to observe the prayers; none was empowered to create them."[7] In other words, the prayers Christians spoke were not spontaneous, individualized prayers like those we think of today. They were common prayers—prayers that the entire church prayed as a community of believers.

In the third century, early monks of the church (called the Desert Fathers) developed a way to follow the apostle Paul's instruction to "pray without ceasing" (1 Thessalonians 5:17, KJV). One group of monks would pray an "office"—a particular prayer at a particular time—and once finished, another group of monks would pray the next office, and then they would turn prayer over to another group, and so on throughout the day and night.[8] In this way, through a community of people, the church was praying without ceasing. Today, this practice continues among Christians who practice fixed-hour common prayer. When you pray the daily office in Chicago at 9:00 a.m., another group of Christians in Denver picks up the mantle an hour later when it becomes 9:00 a.m. mountain time. An hour later, those in Sacramento pray, and so on. Phyllis Tickle notes, "Like relay runners passing a lighted torch, those who do the work of fixed-hour prayer create thereby a continuous cascade of praise before the throne of God."[9]

Despite common prayer's presence in the church since the inception of Christianity and its roots in the Judaism that Jesus practiced, the concept of common prayer may feel foreign to those of us from some Christian denominations.[10] But if we choose to unearth the richness of the practice, we will discover an invaluable way in which God can meet and transform us when we are ashamed, anxious, broken, and afraid.

PRACTICING COMMON PRAYER

At some point or another in our lives, we are going to be the desperate paralyzed man, or the ailing Cardinal Bernardin—we simply will not be able to bring ourselves before God. We will be too overwhelmed by sin or shame, pain or anxiety, fear or doubt. Paul says, "Be patient in trouble, and keep on praying" (Romans 12:12). But how can we do this when we are distressed and just can't find any words or desire to pray? We will need the humility of the paralyzed man and of Cardinal Bernardin to ask that the faith of others carry us before God.

Common prayers allow us that opportunity as we humble ourselves and place ourselves under and within the community of God. We borrow the courage of those who have gone before us. In his book *Letters to a Young Congregation*, Eric Peterson tells a story about a man who was severely depressed and suicidal. Seeing the man's inability to hope, Peterson asked the man if he would "borrow" his faith and his hope—faith that God loved the man and hope that God would allow him to outlive his pain. Even though this man did not himself have the faith necessary to carry him forward in life, as he borrowed someone else's faith, God lifted him out of his despair.[11] Peterson writes,

> This is a foundational aspect of our life together:
> In the alternating seasons of our lives, we find
> ourselves on the giving and the receiving ends of
> the grace of God which compensates and carries,
> borrowing other's faith, bearing one another's
> burdens, fulfilling the law of Christ.[12]

We can enter into community even when we are alone reading a common prayer because common prayers are meant to be said (read) aloud.[13] These prayers are often written with different parts; at times there is a singular reader (signified by plain text), and at others the text is to be read collectively (signified by italicized or bold text). Reading aloud matters. When we say prayers internally, we are easily distracted. So, as insignificant as it may seem initially, using our tongues, mouths, and voices—and especially when we can do so in community—is another way of embodying our faith.

If you're feeling uncertain about where to start with common prayer, the Psalms are a concrete and powerful entry point into this practice. Consider Psalm 51, written by the great King David after his infamous adultery with Bathsheba and murder of Uriah. When the prophet Nathan pointed out David's sin, David had the faith to bring himself before God in prayer (2 Samuel 12); Psalm 51 is his heart-cry to God, seeking forgiveness and restoration. How can we use these words as common prayer? When we have sinned, whether in mundane or spectacular ways, shame may prevent us from believing that God loves us and longs for us to pour our hearts out to him—and that he'll forgive us. But with Psalm 51 at our disposal, we can borrow David's faith and pray on our own behalf:

Have mercy on me, O God,
  because of your unfailing love.
Because of your great compassion,
  blot out the stain of my sins.
Wash me clean from my guilt.
  Purify me from my sin.

PSALM 51:1-2

What a gift these words are. When we are in the midst of brokenness or shame, we can speak out this prayer that David, the one God called a man after his own heart (Acts 13:22), crafted. Speaking these words as our own is a choice of humility, a recognition, as Daniel Taylor put it, that

> sometimes life's troubles may so overwhelm me that I cannot for a time sustain a belief in God's loving concern for me and my fellow creatures. In my humanity I may, like many of my biblical predecessors in the faith, despair or even rage against God. At that point you must believe for me. Do not insist that I still believe. Do not whip the mule that has collapsed under the burden. Do what you can to lighten the burden and wait patiently until I have regained my strength. And someday I will do the same for you.[14]

When we are caught up in our own anxiety or shame, we can spiral and feel alone. Sometimes when I'm trying to go to sleep for the night, a thought will invade my mind and spark worry. I'm not always fully aware of precisely when the spiraling happens, but suddenly I am dreaming up worst-case scenarios and believing them to be perfectly reasonable potential outcomes. In these moments, I feel most alone.

But common prayers remind us that we are not alone—that we are connected not only to a God who loves us but also to the historical body of believers and the community of faith around the world today. Consider this reality: When we pray the Lord's Prayer, we are praying a prayer that Jesus himself taught, that his disciples prayed, and that believers over a span of two thousand years have prayed. Isn't that incredible? When I find myself in a nighttime anxiety spiral, I say the Lord's Prayer aloud (although not loud enough to wake my husband). At first, it allows me to jolt my mind out of the spiral—just as reciting multiplication tables might. As I continue, though, I am brought up above and beyond the spiral. I am reminded of God's reign and goodness (*Father in heaven . . . your Kingdom come*), and then—because the prayer uses plural language (us, our, we)—I realize I am joining in with millions of other Christians over time and place that have prayed this prayer in situations far worse than mine. I find a lot of comfort in this.

In common prayer, we can link arms and hearts with Christians all over the world and throughout time and remember who we are in Christ. We find "not just a poetic genius behind the words but a community in, with, and under the words."[15] In the nights and days and moments when we feel alone, we are joined with an eternal community, each of whom walked their own journey of brokenness, shame, anxiety, and fear.

Common prayer leads me to consider others and think beyond myself, enabling (some might even say pushing) me to pray in ways I would not otherwise pray. They bring me into a place of self-forgetting so that I can focus on others—helping me lend my faith to those who are struggling even as I am leaning on the faith and words of the body of Christ. There is an entire section in the Book of Common Prayer devoted to praying for the people and beauty around us but outside of us. For example,

> For the peace of the world, for the welfare of the Holy Church of God, and for the unity of all peoples, let us pray to the Lord. *Lord have mercy.* . . .

> For our President, for the leaders of the nations, and for all in authority, let us pray to the Lord. *Lord, have mercy.* . . .

> For seasonable weather, and for an abundance of the fruits of the earth, let us pray to the Lord. *Lord, have mercy.* . . .

> For the good earth which God has given us, and for the wisdom and will to conserve it, let us pray to the Lord. *Lord, have mercy.* . . .

> For the aged and infirm, for the widowed and orphans, and for the sick and the suffering, let us pray to the Lord. *Lord, have mercy.* . . .

For the poor and the oppressed, for the
unemployed and the destitute, for prisoners and
captives, and for all who remember and care for
them, let us pray to the Lord. *Lord, have mercy.*[16]

Praying these prayers reminds us of those who are suffering more than we are and whom we can bring before the Lord. Bringing these words before God raises us out of our own muck and mire and helps us apply our faith to others. We become the friends who carried the paralyzed man.

Common prayer also moves our hearts to follow a particularly difficult command of Jesus: to love and pray for our enemies (Matthew 5:43-44). Our brokenness and fear can lead us into unloving postures toward those with whom we disagree or those who have hurt us in some way. We can struggle to forgive someone for pain they've caused. In our modern culture, we can certainly struggle with our feelings even toward those who haven't hurt us but believe differently than we do. But how often do we pray for these kinds of people, those Jesus would say are our enemies? Common prayer can help us pray for our enemies when we don't want to and we cannot formulate the words to forgive. Someone else's words can at least get us started and get us out of our own way. *The Book of Common Prayer* includes the following prayer for our enemies:

O God, the Father of all, whose Son commanded
us to love our enemies: Lead them and us from

prejudice to truth; deliver them and us from
hatred, cruelty, and revenge; and in your good
time enable us all to stand reconciled before you;
through Jesus Christ our Lord. *Amen.*[17]

Lastly, when we are feeling the undertow of our own
brokenness, shame, anxiety, or fear, we probably find joy
elusive. Here, too, common prayer can meet us, providing
prayers of whimsy and joy to enliven us and remind us of
goodness and beauty. The Psalms are, of course, a brilliant
go-to for prayers of praise and exaltation. Also, Ted Loder
wrote a beautiful book of prayers called *Guerrillas of Grace*
that I turn to repeatedly. Here is an example:

> *Praise be to you, O Lord, for life*
> *and for my intense desire to live;*
> *praise be to you for the mystery of love*
> *and for my intense desire to be a lover;*
> *praise be to you for this day*
> *and another chance to live and love.*
>
> *Thank you, Lord,*
> *for friends who stake their claim in my heart,*
> *for enemies who disturb my soul and bump my ego,*
> *for tuba players,*
> *and story tellers,*
> *and trapeze troupes.*

Thank you, Lord,
for singers of songs,
for teachers of songs,
who help me sing along the way,
. . . and for listeners.[18]

Too often in our approach to prayer, we have bought into what the world is selling. We have become so convinced of the desirability of independence and freedom that we have resisted the embrace of the church. We tell ourselves that believers "back then" or of "that sort" do not have the faith and depth of those of us who can pray spontaneously. This is just pride. And this pride is particularly toxic when it comes to facing into our fear, shame, anxiety, and brokenness. Pride tells us not to ask for help and holds us hostage to well-worn patterns. Pride renders us deaf to God's invitations and paralyzes our growth into Christlikeness. Pride denies the truth that "in Christ we, though many, form one body, and each member belongs to all the others" (Romans 12:5, NIV).

But common prayer enters us into communion with believers across the ages and the world and acknowledges that their human struggles mirror and parallel our own. We are not alone in our rebellion against our own humanity and limitedness. We are not alone in our war against the sin that overtakes us, body and mind. And not only are we able to join with believers of the past and the present, we are reminded through common prayer that we are part of an eternal Kingdom, in which Jesus Christ reigns forever and ever. We are not bound to our human ailments forever. A day is coming when our bodies will be made new and our hurts will be healed. Common prayer allows us to keep our eyes fixed on things above, not on earthy things (Colossians 3:2).

PRACTICE GUIDE

As you enter into a practice of common prayer, think of your path forward as one of flexibility and intentionality. As Scot McKnight has said, "Prayer, like love, seeks intimacy through variety in constancy."[19] Skipping around in a prayer book without any routine for days or weeks at a time lacks constancy, and you never really get a feel for the discipline or receive the benefits of common prayer. But praying the same common prayers every day for a year (or even a month) can lack variety. When you allow yourself space for variety while also building in some constancy, this practice will become one that joins you with others in the body of Christ and dispels fear, calms anxiety, and quiets shame.

In pursuit of both flexibility and intentionality, I have found a few helpful approaches. I've incorporated into my routine morning and evening common prayers that greet and then release the day. I am fortified before bed by praying a psalm or a part of a psalm. If I am anxious or fearful, I pray the Lord's Prayer. If I am experiencing doubt, I recite the Nicene Creed (although it is a statement, I make it a prayer). My husband and I go through seasons in which we pray through "A Liturgy for a Husband and Wife: At Close of Day" from Douglas Kaine McKelvey's *Every Moment Holy*. It is beautiful, honest, uniting, and also sometimes hard because it asks that you make amends and ask forgiveness. Most days I also pray spontaneously whatever is on my heart, whether a long paragraph or an indistinct groan. I also change things up depending on the season, like you might with your clothes in your closet.

The most important tip I can give is to pay attention to your soul and what it's really longing for. This is different from what the body wants in order to avoid or cope or numb. In other words, we need to continue noticing our need and recognizing our coping practices. Where do you see unholy leakage, overreaction, defensiveness, or spiraling? Have any of your usual coping practices kicked in? Then, if you don't have the words or faith to bring yourself before Jesus, rely on the church. We are one body in Christ. We are created as interdependent parts—when we are limping along, there are those to hold us up, and when we are strong, there are those we can carry.

A Sample Realistic Day

MORNING

- *Common prayer, asking for grace:* "Lord God, almighty and everlasting Father, you have brought us in safety to this new day: Preserve us with your mighty power, that we may not fall into sin, nor be overcome by adversity; and in all we do, direct us to the fulfilling of your purpose; through Jesus Christ our Lord. *Amen.*"[20]

- *Read:* The One Year Bible daily reading[21]

- *Spontaneous prayer:* journal a prayer for those I love and know and for my own concerns of the day

MEAL TIMES

- *Spontaneous prayer:* give thanks for provision, beauty, and God's presence

RANDOMLY DURING THE DAY
- spontaneous prayers
- the Lord's Prayer
- worship songs

BEDTIME

- *Common or spontaneous prayer:* with my husband, either spontaneous or "A Liturgy for a Husband and Wife: At Close of Day" from Douglas Kaine McKelvey's *Every Moment Holy*

- *Common prayer, confessing sin:* "Most merciful God, we confess that we have sinned against you in thought, word, and deed, by what we have done, and by what we have left undone. We have not loved you with our

114

whole heart; we have not loved our neighbors as ourselves. We are truly sorry and we humbly repent. For the sake of your Son Jesus Christ, have mercy on us and forgive us; that we may delight in your will, and walk in your ways, to the glory of your Name. Amen."[22]

- *Common prayer, asking for protection:* "O God, the life of all who live, the light of the faithful, the strength of those who labor, and the repose of the dead: We thank you for the blessings of the day that is past, and humbly ask you for your protection through the coming night. Bring us in safety to the morning hours; through him who died and rose for us, your Son our Savior Jesus Christ. *Amen.*"[23]

DURING THE NIGHT IF I AWAKE

- *Common prayer:* the Lord's Prayer

When Tempted

O LORD, I am calling to you. Please hurry!
    Listen when I cry to you for help!
Accept my prayer as incense offered to you,
    and my upraised hands as an evening offering.

Take control of what I say, O LORD,
    and guard my lips.
Don't let me drift toward evil
    or take part in acts of wickedness.

Don't let me share in the delicacies
of those who do wrong.

PSALM 141:1-4

In the Shame Spiral

You made all the delicate, inner parts of my body
and knit me together in my mother's womb.
Thank you for making me so wonderfully complex!
Your workmanship is marvelous—how well I
know it.
You watched me as I was being formed in utter
seclusion,
as I was woven together in the dark of
the womb.
You saw me before I was born.
Every day of my life was recorded in your book.
Every moment was laid out
before a single day had passed.

How precious are your thoughts about me,
O God.
They cannot be numbered!
I can't even count them;
they outnumber the grains of sand!
And when I wake up,
you are still with me!

PSALM 139:13-18

Overwhelmed with Anxiety

O God, listen to my cry!
    Hear my prayer!
From the ends of the earth,
    I cry to you for help
    when my heart is overwhelmed.
Lead me to the towering rock of safety,
    for you are my safe refuge,
    a fortress where my enemies cannot reach me.
Let me live forever in your sanctuary,
    safe beneath the shelter of your wings!

PSALM 61:1-4

Overtaken by Fear

Be my light in the darkness, O Lord, and in your great mercy defend me from all perils and dangers; for the love of your only Son, my Savior Jesus Christ. *Amen.*[24]

Prayer Books to Consider

- the book of Psalms
- *Common Prayer: A Liturgy for Ordinary Radicals*
- *An African Prayer Book*
- *The Divine Hours*
- *Guerrillas of Grace: Prayers for the Battle*
- *A Manual of Eastern Orthodox Prayers*
- *Benedictine Daily Prayer*
- *The Book of Common Prayer*

- *Sacred Questions: A Transformative Journey through the Bible*
- *The Little Book of Hours: Praying with the Community of Jesus*[25]

REFLECTION QUESTIONS

1. What has been your experience with common prayer? What makes you nervous about it? What makes you excited?

2. What benefits of common prayer do you see?

3. In what area of your life do you feel the need to borrow someone else's words and/or faith?

4. Who do you know that might need to borrow your words, faith, or hope? How might you offer this to them?

CHAPTER 5

LAUGH OUT LOUD

Laughter is hope's last weapon.

HARVEY COX

In early 2018, part of my job was to oversee the women's ministry at my church. We mostly organized and ran classes—everything from Bible studies to topical or stage-of-life classes to spiritual-formation experiences. But for some reason, we didn't host events for women too often. As I looked at our church, I realized that even though the women in each class were bonded together, there wasn't a sense of a broader community. How could we bring all the women in our community together?

Then I had a flash of an idea that to this day I believe was from the Holy Spirit. What if we hosted a night of laughter? A chance for enjoying one another in community, of being silly and releasing our stresses and just . . . laughing? As I brought the idea to my boss and our team, I was clear on one thing: I didn't want to set any goal for the night except to laugh. If women eventually got connected, took a next step, or joined a small group, I'd be ecstatic. But at this event, we would practice being present, laughing together, and sharing in joy.

A team of volunteers and I dove into planning the event. Would we tell jokes? Play pranks? Hire a comedian? Was making people laugh something we could do for two hours? We brainstormed (and laughed a lot) and came up with a plan we were all looking forward to.

And then our world fell apart. An article came out with the news that our senior pastor of forty years had engaged in several instances of sexual misconduct during his tenure. The allegations were specific and damning. Although he denied them, within a month's time he resigned, and our church was left heartbroken, confused, and angry. We didn't know what was true, who to believe, or how to carry on now that the man we had held in such high regard, who had been leading us for so long, was suddenly gone and disgraced. Surely he would repent for whatever wrongs he committed. After all, this is what he stood for, taught, and expected from others.

The fallout continued for months. Eventually the elder board of the church, the teaching pastor, and the executive pastor all resigned. Words can't adequately express the heartache and extensive damage we all experienced. I was personally deeply impacted and am still working through the pain of it all. But in the midst of the turmoil, our women's-event team found ourselves facing a difficult question: Do we still hold our night of laughter event, or do we cancel it because now is not the time to laugh?

I prayed and considered at the very least delaying the event. We couldn't possibly promote fun and laughter under these circumstances, right? People might think we were being dismissive of the seriousness of the situation. The more I prayed, though, the more convinced I became that laughter was precisely what we needed. In such painful times for our church, we needed to be together and remember where our hope resided—and that our connection to Christ and to one another was reason to be joyful. Laughing together wouldn't mean we didn't care. Laughter would be our protest against suffering and those who caused it.[1]

We moved ahead. We announced our event. I watched registrations go from 10 to 100 to 500. When we settled into the room together for our evening, nearly 700 women had shown up to laugh. We blew bubbles, played silly games, told riddles and stories, and watched a few fun videos. We sang happy birthday and handed out prizes. We laughed so hard, tears ran down our faces. And we listened to the story of a woman who laughed even in the midst of the heartache of losing her husband.[2]

God knew what he was doing months earlier when he

planted the idea for a night of laughter in my heart and mind. Indeed, he "gave us laughter to relieve the strain of living in a fallen world."[3] We all need laughter in the midst of our brokenness, shame, fear, and anxiety, because there are so many gaps between our expectations and reality. So much of life—most of it, even—is characterized by uncertainty, insecurity, paradox, hypocrisy. How can we bear such things? How can people—even people we love—cause so much pain? Well, we know exactly how when we examine ourselves and humanity, yet we still are so hurt and quite often surprised by the paradox.

If you're a more serious type of person (like me), you may feel some resistance to this idea that laughter can be a spiritual practice, something that can have a profound impact on the darkest parts of our souls. Laughing seems frivolous and unspiritual, even undignified. I don't laugh easily, just so you know. I can make other people laugh, but actually laughing myself is a discipline I've had to develop and practice. When I went away to college, I was surprised to discover that people laughed out loud. In my experience, laughing was something you reserved for family dinners or gatherings. You wouldn't just laugh in a public space or with people you barely knew. One time, when a new friend burst out laughing at a television show we were watching in her room, I almost asked if she was okay.

After a while, I began to realize that I was a very serious person. Something about my personality kept me from laughing too often or out loud. Years later, when I became a lawyer, my seriousness deepened. Lawyers don't laugh. (Really, they don't. We are a pretty serious and stressed-out bunch.)

About eight years into my legal career, I became a Christian. I was so relieved to have been rescued by God from a life that seemed to be spinning out of control that my seriousness deepened even further. I wanted to be devoted and follow God as best I could. And although the Bible has lots to say about joy, I never connected joy with laughter or had the faintest sense that laughter might be important to my spiritual growth and walk with Jesus. After all, many of the mature Christians I knew appeared quite serious.

On the other hand, I came to know several people who had walked through very difficult seasons of loss—and still, they laughed. In fact, these people had laughs that other people would talk about—"Oh, is he the one with that deep laugh?" "She's the one that laughs, right?" Laughing with abandon *and* Christian. Very interesting.

Questioning the propriety of laughing Christians is not new. The early fathers "often assumed that it [laughter] had no worthwhile place in the Christian community."[4] John Chrysostom, a venerated theologian and saint, argued that based on Scripture, Christ never laughed and that we would be more bonded to God through tears and sorrow.[5] As theology professor and author Brian Edgar wrote,

The Christian tradition has developed a long list of objections to humor. It has been seen as offensive, aggressive, excluding, irresponsible, hedonistic, mocking, undignified, frivolous, spiteful, madness, anarchic, unworthy of God, and foolish.[6]

Of course—to paraphrase the apostle Paul (1 Corinthians 10:23)—not all laughter is beneficial or useful. We should be on guard against the impulse to laugh at jokes that tear people down or diminish them. But we should not dismiss the reality that laughter is very, well, human. As Edgar tells us, "to be human is to be humorous and this humor is, along with all aspects of the person, to be redeemed and a part of the future," life in God's Kingdom.[7]

So why is there such little laughter in the Bible, particularly in the New Testament? As I've studied, I've found two helpful explanations.[8] First, the Gospels were not biographies, and their writers weren't interested in sharing everything about Jesus.[9] They don't reference Jesus using the bathroom, but given that he was fully human, we can assume he did. Similarly, given the humanness of laughter, and Jesus' humanity, we can also assume he laughed. Second, we can reasonably assume that Jesus' stories and parables—full of statements and questions that turned the patterns of the world on their head (the last shall be first, etc.)—elicited laughter and astonishment.[10]

In 2017, about nine years after I became a Christian, I began dating and then married (all in the same year) my husband. He loves to laugh and has a great sense of humor. He studied comedy as a craft with Second City in Chicago;

he knows how jokes work and what makes something funny. He laughs when he's alone, and sometimes things he thinks make him laugh out loud! As I observed him, I started to reflect on two things: *Why I didn't laugh more* and *why I didn't feel like laughing more.* I began to notice that I would hold back laughter. Laughter required a kind of vulnerability that I didn't like. I was worried my face would contort in weird ways or that I would snort. Our bodies, after all, spontaneously do things that we have no real control over:

It starts with the face, with a smile, then that smiling turns into laughter. It involves the use of fifteen different facial muscles. Something really peculiar happens when we begin laughing: our larynx, the little muscular organ in our throat that we sometimes call the voice box, half closes. This tightening of our throat makes it very difficult for us to breathe and because we are now at risk of not getting enough of that sweet, sweet oxygen we seem to like so much, we begin gasping for air. That is where the sound of laughter comes from, literally the sound of laughter is simply us GASPING FOR AIR! If we continue, the struggle for oxygen will activate our tear ducts and we'll start tearing up, maybe even crying.[11]

The health benefits of laughter have been well-studied and documented: reducing our sensitivity to physical pain and our need for painkillers in recovering from surgery; lowering blood pressure and blood sugar; relieving anxiety and depression; and improving our immune system, among many other things.[12] Laughter also helps to "relieve stress, overcome tragedy, cope with disappointment, elevate mood, encourage optimism, and create social bonds."[13]

But what does laughter mean for our places of brokenness, shame, anxiety, and fear? When we laugh, we are professing with our bodies that we aren't taking ourselves so seriously. We are not thinking of ourselves more highly than we ought. We are leaning into and embracing our humanity. When Paul wrote to the Romans about how to offer their lives as a living sacrifice to God, he instructed them to "laugh with your happy friends when they're happy; share tears when they're down" (Romans 12:15, MSG). Laughing with your happy friends is a way of placing your whole life—including your body—before God as an offering. Even Martin Luther, who I never imagined to be the laughing type, used laughter therapy when he pastored those with depression.[14] Karl Barth was known as a humorist who "saw laughter as a recognition of human frailty."[15] When I withhold laughter when it springs up naturally, I am rebelling against how I've been created. The lightness and joy of laughter is a gift of our humanity, a gift from our Creator, who knows how heavy our lives can be. When we choose to accept that gift, we find that the things encumbering us suddenly seem smaller and that God joins us in the midst of the joy.

Have you ever experienced the pure joy of uncontrollable laughter? It always seems to happen at the most inopportune times, when laughter is not socially acceptable—formal dinners, funerals, during a speech. Just recently, at my step-father's funeral, I thought I'd have to get up and leave the service for fear of bursting into laughter. The full range of my emotions was close to the surface . . . and the priest was conducting the whole thing so oddly! His tone, his manner—everything was so strange, my mom was struggling to contain her laughter, too; when she glanced at me, I thought we were both going to lose it. Yes, we were sad— so sad. But something about the absurdity of the whole thing led us right to the brink of overwhelming laughter. (It turns out that most everyone else there experienced the same thing—we all held it together until the luncheon, when we collectively cried with laughter.)

This spontaneous, pee-your-pants laughter reflects a heart that is—even if only momentarily—free and unencumbered by shame, anxiety, and fear. And a heart that is free is open and vulnerable. I had not experienced God's presence with me at the moments surrounding my step-father's death like I really wanted to—when he breathed his last breath or when we drove home from the hospital and sat around telling stories. But at the luncheon as I laughed, I imagined my stepfather laughing with us. Pictures of him at various points in my life flashed through my mind. I was tenderhearted and open—and there I felt God's peace and presence. The stress my entire body carried and the fear that was lurking in me dissipated. The first few words of Julian of Norwich's famous quote washed over me: "All shall be well, and all shall be well and all manner of thing shall be well."[16]

Why do we struggle with laughter? The usual culprits— worry and fear—are at work to stymie joy, even more so than any pain or grief. This reality makes me sad because I can't imagine my anxiety and fear going away anytime soon, given that they've been with me most, if not all, of my life. But I'd like to laugh freely and uncontrollably more often and be increasingly free of the anxiety that so often hangs on me.

If you don't feel like you're good at laughter, I have good news for you, as a fellow struggler. Learning to laugh and find the joy in life is something that a person can get better at through practice. According to psychologist Brian King, "Like any behavior, laughter takes practice. We did not learn how to walk on our first try. We didn't learn how to speak with our first drooly mumblings, and we don't learn to laugh without the right socialization and practice."[17] So if you find that the fears and anxieties of your life are hard to shake, start seeking out ways to practice laughter.

PRACTICE GUIDE

Laughter isn't something you have to manufacture. Our world and lives are full of ways we can spark laughter and joy, and each of us can figure out what works for us. Let me share a few that have resonated deeply with me.

In the winter of 2019, through an amazing Christian ministry called Safe Families, my husband and I had the privilege of opening our home to host two siblings (a five-year-old boy and a two-year-old girl) for nearly three months while their mom found a home and a job. My husband and I have three grown children in their twenties (and no grandkids yet), so it had been quite a while since we had little ones around. But, putting aside the fact that we nearly died from exhaustion because we weren't used to so much energy, we had an amazing experience and fell head over heels in love with these kids.

And you know what we did more than usual? We laughed. The body noises, the uninhibited dances and wiggles, the crazy new moves we came up with during family dance parties—all of it cracked us up. We colored, cut up paper, "played" ping-pong, tickled little toes, sang in the bathtub, opened Christmas presents, swung and slid down slides, and jumped on trampolines and inflatable slides at the bouncy house. Even eating dinner was fun. There was no end to their energy, and nearly everything we did made us laugh.

The thing about it was, I never felt self-conscious with them. If they wanted me to sing a silly song, I did, and it brought me great joy. I laughed with abandon and stayed present in the moment (until my energy started dipping ahead of their bedtime!). Our kids are back with their mom now, but they still come and visit once a month so we can give their mom a little break. And these are the sweetest, most fun, most laugh-filled times we have. In these moments, I best understand some of Jesus' words:

> I'm telling you, once and for all, that unless you return to square one and start over like children, you're not even going to get a look at the kingdom, let alone get in. Whoever becomes simple and elemental again, like this child, will rank high in God's kingdom. What's more, when you receive the childlike on my account, it's the same as receiving me.
>
> MATTHEW 18:3-5, MSG

If you struggle with laughter, my first suggestion is to be around kids! They force you out of your comfort zone but still manage to allow you to feel completely at ease as you act goofy and play like a child. When they laugh, you can't help but laugh too.

My second suggestion is to dance! From time to time, even when the kids aren't here, my husband and I and our girls will have our own little dance parties to loosen up and bring joy back into the room. In the Bible, dance is both a reflection of and a trigger for joy and laughter. Spiritual teacher Barbara Holmes explores dance's especially "prominent role in the black church," where "it affords a worshipping community a way to share in the spiritual journey."[18] She provides a revolutionary perspective on the relationship between dance and joy, pointing out that "some scholars suggest that the words *rejoice* and *dance* are the same in Aramaic, the language Jesus and the disciples spoke."[19] If we replace *rejoice* with *dance* in the New Testament, we see Jesus suggest that we dance when people hate us and mock us because we follow him (Luke 6:23).[20] We also see the shepherd, the woman who lost her coin, and the father in the story of the Prodigal Son rejoice (dance) when they find what has been lost (Luke 15:6, 9, 25).

Another source of laughter for me? Games! Our family loves cards, board games, darts, ping-pong, bags (or cornhole), basketball, mini-golf—pretty much anything. This was always true in my family growing up as well. Most of my memories of laughing hysterically have involved playing games. Grandma failing to offer a single clue in Taboo before the one-minute timer runs out. My then-eight-year-old sister's drawing skills approximating a Rorschach ink blob instead of a snowblower. Playing the speed card game Spoons, and the mad rush for a spoon when someone falls over and knocks drinks and food off the table. And if you're looking for an easy game guaranteed to help you practice laughter, I can't recommend Apples to Apples more.

Your practices can be anything that helps you feel unhindered enough to laugh, and they're particularly important to pursue when you're feeling battered down by shame, anxiety, and everything else. Here are a few more ideas:

- tell dumb "dad jokes";
- lip-sync songs (or do karaoke!);

- set up some silly competitions (like home Olympics or throwing cards into a basket);
- blow bubbles;
- play tag; or
- Hula-Hoop.®

REFLECTION QUESTIONS

1. What connection do you see between laughter and your relationship with God?

2. Consider a time when laughter brought healing to your relationships or to your heart. What was that experience like?

3. What makes you laugh, and how can you do that more?

4. How has laughter helped you in moments of temptation, shame, anxiety, or fear?

CHAPTER 6

DIG IN THE DIRT

Every suburban flower garden and every rural allotment has
the potential of a two-way mirror: to bring eternity right
down into our own backyard, and to open up in our own
small worlds something of the very mind and heart of God.

MARGARET SILF

*W*hen God created human beings, he could have put us anywhere, in any imaginable (to him) location and context. But he planted a Garden with all kinds of trees with leaves and fruits, and a river running through it, and placed us there. Not only that, but God gave us this Garden and all that was in it (Genesis 1:29). The man and woman were to enjoy what came from the ground—the looks, feels, smells, tastes, and sounds. The trees in the Garden God planted nourished their bodies, sparked their taste buds, and dazzled their eyes and noses with beauty and aroma.

God's intention, though, was that humanity would work the Garden and take care of it (Genesis 2:15). It wouldn't

just self-propagate and magically stay healthy and beautiful. They were to dig in the dirt, fostering the growth and
maturation of the plants, grains, and fruit trees. They were
to stroll through the Garden and notice how to best care
for what God had planted. (I can't quite figure out how
they did this. I need to look everything up on YouTube
so I know when to weed and water and how to trim and
harvest. Maybe God gave them detailed instructions.)

From the beginning, humans were not just connected
to the ground—formed out of it and placed in it—but
also intended to cultivate the ground and all it produced.
Digging in the dirt is a fundamental element of what it
means to be human.

The more I think about this creation story, the more I
understand why I feel so connected to God and to myself
when I'm sitting in the grass, hands in the dirt, remov-
ing debris and weeds from around my tomato plants.
Remember the story of Moses and the burning bush, and
how God told him to remove his sandals? "'Do not come
any closer,' the LORD warned. 'Take off your sandals, for
you are standing on holy ground'" (Exodus 3:5). I once
heard a pastor suggest that God didn't want Moses to
come closer until he took his shoes off not because his
sandals were dirty but so that Moses' feet, his body, could
touch the holiness (meaning set apart-ness[1]). God didn't
want any barrier to come between them.

The stories of Scripture assume that human hands
and bodies are at work with the earth. This is why the

law included rules like, "When you harvest the crops of your land, do not harvest the grain along the edges of your fields, and do not pick up what the harvesters drop. It is the same with your grape crop—do not strip every last bunch of grapes from the vines, and do not pick up the grapes that fall to the ground. Leave them for the poor and the foreigners living among you" (Leviticus 19:9-10). And this is why Jesus told parables about trees, scattered seed, crops in barns, the mustard seed, the lost sheep, and the evil farmer. These concepts were common for Jesus' disciples.

But in our modern (postmodern or post-postmodern) Western world, many of us rarely touch the earth. We are blocked off from the holiness. When we walk, we wear shoes. When we sit, it is in chairs or on blankets or towels. When we pull weeds, we wear gloves and kneel on garden pads. We can hardly recognize the fruits and vegetables we see at the grocery store, let alone know how to grow them or cultivate the soil so that they will grow. Workers cut our flowers and place them by the hundreds in black bins at the store. Meanwhile, our hands type on keyboards, swipe screens, and push virtual buttons. Our eyes scroll electronic photos, virtual worlds, and the make-believe of television and movies. None of this is necessarily bad, but it certainly has separated us from the earth. And, in this way, from our humanity. We don't all need to go out and become farmers, but we must consider what we've lost by distancing ourselves from the actual things of the earth—the things that are dirty, prickly, unknown, and unseen.

Why is connection to and cultivation of the earth so important to being human? Consider for a moment all the things in your life over which you have no or very little control—what happens to your own body, how other people drive, your kids and their choice of job or spouse, the economy, the weather, and a million other things. Even your own responses to situations seem to be predetermined by traumas you've experienced in the past or biological conditions that you didn't have the chance to say yes or no to. And consider how we try to wrangle all of these uncontrollable happenings without success, to the detriment of our own souls. We fear death, so we worry about it, then we shame ourselves for worrying about it when God tells us we need not fear or worry. We are ashamed of our brokenness, so we hide and cope and confess. Then we do it all over again.

Tending to the earth is the way God gave us to ground ourselves in our humanity and thus in him. We are creatures only because he is creator. And as we've talked about before, we are in rebellion when we fail to acknowledge our creatureliness and instead seek to be God. Few things help us lean into our humanity more than planting and caring for a garden or tending to the earth that has been given to us.

I used to think God used my attempts to engage with nature to show me my utter lack of ability to make things grow. I have no control and thus am humbled to my proper place. But what I have come to realize is that when it comes to the piece of earth I have been given (and this may change over a lifetime), I have been given the precise amount of control. In the garden, there is nothing I can do alone—but if I do nothing at all, the ground will not produce as it is able.

God invites us into a partnership in this life—to walk and work with him to bring about the fullness of his Kingdom (Matthew 28:18-20). We can find no better place to experience the reality of this partnership firsthand than in the garden. I can come to know my role and God's role. I can realize that these roles are different and that only God can do certain things—allow the sun to shine and the rain to fall—but also that he has invited me to do certain things. If we do not foster the soil, remove the weeds, and cultivate our plants through thinning and pruning, God won't either. That is our job. He will wait until we participate and partner with him. If we decide not to, that's up to us—and the peppermint we planted will take over not just the garden, but entire swaths of the yard.

Over the years, I have learned that I need to build in quiet times and spaces to restore myself—to be at my best, able to love others well, exercise patience and compassion, and be attuned to God's presence. When I have had too many days in a row with intense meetings or constant social interactions and have failed to set aside restoration time, I begin to feel unhinged and untethered. My anxiety levels are high. I can't focus. I can't sit still, and I find myself holding my head and rubbing my temples. My emotional tiredness overwhelms me, and tears push against the insides of my eyes, ready to burst out at the slightest inconvenience. My unholy leakage is on full display during these times—I am irritable, exhausted, and apparently don't have the internal resources to muster kindness or patience. Taking a nap or sitting alone doesn't really seem to help—my body isn't what needs rest.

One day after many weeks of a full house, social gatherings, and a busy meeting schedule at work, I realized that God felt distant. I was turning to him more as a magic genie who could release me from my discomfort rather than seeing him as a loving person whose presence I desired. In the midst of my funk, I noticed that my vegetable garden and a nearby flower garden seemed to be filling up with maple samaras (you know, those helicopter things that fall from the trees). Pretty soon I would have little maple trees sprouting up all over, sucking the nutrients from my bell pepper plants and wild flowers. In fact, some had already begun to dig their way into the ground. I needed to lift all of these whirlybirds out of my mulch and get rid of them, but I couldn't rake because the space was too small and the plants would be in the way. The only way would be to pick them up one by one.

I sat down next to the garden, feeling the tickle of grass on the backs of my knees, and picked out a single samara. How many of these had I touched and thrown into the air as a kid? How many had I swept off our driveway or pried out of the cracks in the car where they'd blown in overnight? How had I never considered the miracle of life each one held within it? This minuscule thing would grow, if allowed, into an enormous tree that would provide shade, shelter dozens of kinds of birds, clean the air of carbon dioxide and release oxygen, and even reduce the stress levels of those living nearby. I dropped the samara into my landscaping bucket and picked up another. Worms and pill bugs (roly-polys) squirmed away as I uncovered them. Ants scurried about. I started to feel a lightness in my forehead and noticed I was smiling. Peace dropped into my chest. And I felt less anxious. Having my hands on the things of the earth grounded me. I could take fuller breaths, and the frazzled, floating feeling left me. Simple prayers of gratitude escaped my lips: "Thank you, Lord. Thank you." When I finished, there were a few left here and there, but my vegetable plants were no longer surrounded—light and water could get through.

Gardening and tending to the earth also opens us to God by allowing us to begin to see death as part of the rhythm of creation. As we scoop handfuls of dirt with our hands, recognizing all that has come and gone in such a small piece of earth, we are stripped of the illusion that any individual life (including our own) can escape death. We are faced with the universality of mortality, and if we are present and attuned, our own mortality. Acceptance of this reality takes time—many seasons turning the dirt over to really internalize. We are all in such denial that we are moving toward death that it takes nearly all of our life to come to terms with that ultimate truth. This, Ronald Rolheiser argues, is because the infinite within us, made as we are in the divine and infinite image, does not "sit calmly" in the finiteness of this life.[2] But the more we remain in denial, the less we are able to be present to God. Our fear distracts and separates us from the gift of life and the present.

My stepfather of thirty-four years, Dorsey, was a quadriplegic, and although he lived a remarkable life, his body got to the point where it couldn't take any more. He developed problems breathing, and over time the doctors could not stabilize him and keep the airway open. Nurses had to constantly revive him just to keep him alive. And so we waited for the inevitable. My mom slept in the hospital chair for nearly six weeks. Then, one night, he slid away from us. This man who had lived so fully and had endured so much physical injury and hardship was gone. He is gone. He could not sustain himself. We could not—and doctors could not—keep the breath God had given him in him.

If you have experienced death up close like this before, you know the immense sadness, absence, and fear that accompanies it. In these moments, death feels surprising and inevitable all at once. Maybe you have felt God in these moments, present and palpable. I really didn't. I wanted to, wanted to remind my family of his nearness—and even more, I wanted to sense it myself. What I felt instead was fear, anxiety, absence, and strangeness in the face of the incomprehensibility and finality of death.

As we neared the date of the funeral, I noticed that I

was leaking emotionally. I was losing patience. Every sound grated on my nerves. I could feel myself losing my footing and being overtaken. There was grief for sure; Dorsey had been a forceful figure in my life. But lurking just under the surface was fear and anxiety about death itself.

It was early fall. All the harbingers of winter were there—the fallen leaves, small branches from trees, wilted leaves, browning plants. But the dirt still beckoned me to come out and dig my hands in. Without saying much to anyone, I went into the shed and got a big, orange Home Depot bucket and some scissors. I sat down on the sidewalk in front of the house, which was lined with overgrown hostas that needed to be trimmed back for the winter. Their soil was covered in debris from the fallen leaves. I took each green leaf, feeling the sturdiness of it and its stalk. Then, wondering if I was really doing the right thing, I began to cut, one at a time, studying the way the leaves looked like they had tried to heal themselves after being bitten through by slimy slugs. I dug around each plant to pick up sticks, stems, and rocks that hid under the long leaves. As my fingernails filled with the dirt of the earth, a phrase ran over and over in my mind: *You are dust, and to dust you shall return* (see Genesis 3:19). How strange and sad. How humbling and sobering. These complex bodies that plague us, serve us, and rule over us in so many ways began as dust and will return to that state again. And yet, sprinkled among the dead leaves as I looked and touched were sprouts. I hadn't ever noticed that new things come up even in the fall. The human condition is to end in death. But the human condition *in Christ* is to be restored and given new and eternal life (Ephesians 2:4-7). The dirt that I dug my hands into was cool to the touch and was filled with earthworms, leafy particles, minuscule rocks, and stubborn roots. This dirt was sustaining so many different forms of life. Playing in the dirt—turning it over in my hands and letting it run through my fingers—felt oddly intimate. My muscles relaxed a bit. I breathed in the earthy smell, and air reached the depths of my lungs for the first time in a while. There was peace and acceptance.

My internal self is always so disintegrated, it seems—partially here and partially there. Fear and shame and anxiety have their way so much of the time, distracting and sending my thoughts in a thousand different directions. But when I've got my hands in the dirt and my skin touching the earth, I am integrated again. As writer Janice Elsheimer describes, I experience here, like nowhere else, a oneness with my Creator.[3] There is hardly anything more tempting in the midst of such an experience than to try to come up with some clever spiritual metaphor to describe it. I think I'm supposed to try to figure out what the dirt means, what the digging represents, or what all the debris could stand for in order for the experience to mean something. It's hard to simply experience the oneness and take it to be what it is. But right there in my little plot of land, in the dirt, there is creation, life, death, and resurrection.

Worries and fears in these intimate, connected moments are irrelevant. The present takes precedence.

Shame seems to be particularly responsive to the practice of digging in the dirt. I think this is so for a couple reasons. You're never really done working in the garden. The branches of a trimmed tree grow back, vegetables must be watered and harvested, weeds sprout up every day, and you can never seem to pick up every dead leaf. And "failure" is a frequent occurrence. Certain seeds won't grow, you'll overwater a particular plant, you'll pull a healthy stem instead of a weed, or all of the above. In a culture where perfectionism is a high value, our imperfectness can be fertile ground for shame for many of us. Yet imperfection is, in some sense, the essence of gardening. If you talk to anyone who plants and cultivates the earth, they will tell you how much trial and error there is with just about everything—growing seeds, keeping away pests, transplanting, composting, all of it. It's art, not science. Failure is inevitable, incompleteness is integral. Of course, this is true in life generally, but practicing in a smaller setting (the garden), allows us to embrace these things more and more often in our larger setting (life).

You don't have to have a yard to dig in the dirt. Community gardens, indoor gardens, and minigardens are all becoming more and more popular for those who live in urban areas or apartment settings. Before I had a yard, I grew herbs inside in little pots I kept by the kitchen window. I never harvested them or ate them (although I intended to) because I over- and then under-watered a few. Then one of my cats apparently enjoyed oregano too much to let that continue to grow. But even this experience filled me with the same kind of peace and grounding in God that a larger garden setting gives. No matter how I am able to dig in the dirt, as I use my body as it was intended to tend and cultivate the earth, my heart is better able to receive God's love for me and share that with others. My anxiety and fear levels go down. I see shame coming a mile away and can walk through it without going down the spiral. I am, as Paul instructed, offering my body as a living sacrifice.

PRACTICE GUIDE

What you're able to do to cultivate and tend the earth depends on where you are and the land you have to work with. You may have to get creative if you live in an urban area. There are parks, forest preserves, and even beaches where you can at least sit on the earth or lie on your back and feel it under you. The key is to remember the purpose: to open yourself to God's presence and healing. The temptation will be to try to force yourself to have a spiritual experience or develop some fancy metaphors. But just be and feel. And wait to see how it may ground you and open your heart. Here are some ideas:

- trim or prune a tree;
- plant some flowers;

- chop wood;
- clear out a flower bed;
- grow vegetables (inside or out);
- walk barefoot;
- rake leaves, pick them up, smell them;
- peel a potato or a cucumber;
- grow an herb garden; or
- go for a walk and notice and touch the different kinds of trees, plants, and flowers you see.

REFLECTION QUESTIONS

1. How connected have you been to the earth during your life? How would you describe your experience?

2. What hesitations do you have about digging in the dirt?

3. How have you experienced God in nature in the past?

4. Do you feel intimacy with God when connected to the ground and the dirt? Why do you think that is?

CHAPTER 7

ENCOURAGE OTHERS

Just as each of us has one body with many members,
and these members do not all have the same function,
so in Christ we, though many, form one body,
and each member belongs to all the others.

ROMANS 12:4-5, NIV

A good friend of mine once posted a picture of his son jumping off a diving board into a lake somewhere in Wisconsin. I think I saw it as I scrolled through Instagram some evening. The picture caught my attention. I centered it on my phone. I looked at the kid's face. This was his first time jumping by himself. He was smiling, but there was also a tinge of fear behind his eyes. He was tan, and the water was clear and flat. The sun was shining, and it was a beautiful day. Not too far away from the spot in the water where the kid would land was his dad (my friend). My friend's arms were extended fully over his head, his hands in fists, a sign of victory and celebration. His mouth was open in an O shape as if he had just witnessed the most glorious, unexpected event. Happiness and encouragement radiated from his face and body language. He could not have been more proud of or more excited about his son's courage and confidence. Even now, years later, that picture is burned in my brain as a display of encouragement in its purest form.

I must start this chapter with a confession: Encouraging others is very difficult for me. I'm not 100 percent sure why, but when someone I know accomplishes something great—especially in my own areas of perceived expertise—my natural instinct is not to immediately celebrate them. My natural instinct is to withhold. When someone expresses a view that's different from mine, my natural instinct is not to lean in and seek to understand but to become further entrenched in my own view and dismissive of theirs. I am apt to cease to listen or offer the benefit of the doubt, even though I'd never say so in the moment. This less-than-great trait of mine is particularly pronounced when I'm feeling fear and anxiety. I begin to compare myself, my abilities, my family, and my accomplishments with those of others. And this is the really hard part to share: In this fear and anxiety of not being good enough, I elevate myself above others and take a position of superiority instead of humility. This elevation of myself is unholy leakage. It's a sign of trouble in my soul.

I'm ashamed to share all this, and I'm still working

through possible causes (and solutions). Two conditions I have identified, though, include a scarcity mindset and a stingy heart. Somehow I have come to fear that there is only so much good to go around. So if a friend receives accolades on her writing, I sense that I cannot. I don't think there are enough accolades in the world for me if someone else receives them. And if anyone does receive accolades, it should be me, not someone else. I don't believe any of this crosses my mind consciously, but it's there.

I want to hide this lack of generosity of spirit in myself. It really bothers me. Yet it's my default mode—and at least one of the reasons I need to practice encouragement as a discipline. In some ways, I'm a product of our culture (scarcity mindset), and in other ways I'm just human (stingy heart).

Until I became a Christian, encouragement wasn't a concept I really ran into much. I've been encouraged in my life at various points by parents and teachers for sure, but encouragement as a gift one can practice and get better at is a newer thought for me. And I don't think I'm the only one. The idea of building up others has become increasingly foreign in our culture. Our world is becoming more and more self-focused, image-obsessed, and willing to cancel anyone who makes even the slightest mistake.

Good values underlie cancel culture in its purest form— justice for the injured and accountability for those who hurt. And social media has allowed individuals with no power to rely on themselves instead of the government or organizations to call the powerful to account. Several sex predators have been caught and stopped due to a call for accountability on social media. These are all good things. But we can take it too far. We are so practiced at judging, condemning, and punishing. Rare are the news stories of redemption and restoration. In fact, rare are the news stories in which redemption or restoration is even an option. The public social-media arena has become the Roman Colosseum, where lions rush in to kill and destroy and you are given a thumbs up or thumbs down by a collective that knows little, if anything, about you. Whatever wrongs an offender has committed must be exposed; they should no longer receive support or have jobs or a platform for their ideas or talents. Second chances and redemption are not in view. Cancel culture leaves no room for the notion that people can change. It assumes that anyone who says or does something that offends must forever be defined by those words or actions.

We must take care not to simply destroy individuals and reduce them to an ideology. It separates them from the body (or members from the community) and tells them they are no longer wanted, no longer valued. What happens when someone says something "offensive" in a postchurch coffee connect? Does that congregant get canceled? Do entire groups of people get canceled from certain churches because they hold opinions or say things that others find offensive, insensitive, uncomfortable, or contrary to their views? Or does the church embrace them, listen to their stories, and lead them with gentleness to Jesus Christ? Do Christians build up with love and in love, or do they tear down with judgment and condemnation?

Paul's words in his letter to the Roman churches—churches that were filled with people of different backgrounds and statuses—make me think that what we deal with today has been happening for a long time:

Love from the center of who you are; don't fake it. Run for dear life from evil; hold on for dear life to good. Be good friends who love deeply; practice playing second fiddle. . . .

Bless your enemies; no cursing under your breath. Laugh with your happy friends when they're happy; share tears when they're down. Get along with each other; don't be stuck-up. Make friends with nobodies; don't be the great somebody.

Don't hit back; discover beauty in everyone. If you've got it in you, get along with everybody. Don't insist on getting even; that's not for you to do. "I'll do the judging," says God. "I'll take care of it."

Our Scriptures tell us that if you see your enemy hungry, go buy that person lunch, or if he's thirsty, get him a drink. Your generosity will surprise him with goodness. Don't let evil get the best of you; get the best of evil by doing good.

ROMANS 12:9-10, 14-21, MSG

Oh, how we need people who will live this way. Instead of building each other up, we tear each other down. All of this has found its way into the church. So how do we instead become people of encouragement?

We can tend to think of encouragement as saying a word here or there to a friend or colleague to spur them on in their personal or work pursuits. Perhaps you arrived at this chapter and thought you were in for a short break because this one is easy! Maybe you, like me, have thought of encouragement as a somewhat insubstantial gift—like a compliment from your mom or grandmother. You know what I mean: When they tell us something is great, we take it with a grain of salt because, well, they're our moms or grandmas. They almost *have* to say nice stuff.

In actuality, encouragement as a practice might be the most difficult of those I've written about so far. Indeed, encouragement takes great discipline and intention because it is no less than being Christ to one another. Encouragement is a "total commitment to be God's instrument in other people's lives."[1] It is honoring others above ourselves. It is placing our needs beneath the needs of others. It is being fully present to one another. It is foregoing our need to be seen and known so that another can be seen and known. It is allowing thoughts and feelings of ours to go unexpressed for the good of others. It is withholding opinions and our desire to be right. It is getting out of ourselves and becoming more interested in someone else. It is a "conscious commitment to promote other people's welfare."[2]

We have left this kind of sacrifice and discipline behind us. In fact, as a society, we seem to have become convinced that being our authentic selves and expressing our "truth" trumps all other values we may otherwise hold. As author and psychologist Larry Crabb has said so poignantly,

> Our values revolve too much around ideals like openness, authenticity, transparency, assertion, fulfillment, and genuineness. And we tend to regard as outdated concepts like sacrificial giving, self-discipline, self-denying love, obedience, and willing endurance. Yet, Paul reminds us that we no longer live in the lusts of the flesh and the desires of the mind; we were dead but have been made alive, quickened by his power and enabled to live obedient lives (Ephesians 2:1-10).[3]

As Christians, we have been set apart and equipped by the Spirit to act different from the culture around us—not to conform, as Paul would say, to the patterns of the world (Romans 12:2, NIV). This means that we are to go against the grain of cancelation, vilification, and condemnation. We are to withhold our opinions and feelings for the sake of others, even if we think we're right. We are to think through and discern how to confront injustice and wrongdoing so that even such offenders are treated with honor and love. This is true even if we ourselves will be persecuted as a result. I am convinced that this kind of encouragement is impossible without empathy—and that empathy is what we are really lacking. Only by developing empathy and allowing that empathy to be expressed as encouragement can we redirect ourselves and commit to the values Christ exemplified and taught. (An important caveat: I am not suggesting that the victims of abuse are to reach out to abusers and encourage them. Any kind of interaction that a victim of abuse might have with their abuser would need to be discussed with and guided by professionals, prioritizing the safety of the victim.)

Our first task, then, is to grow in empathy, because out of an overflow of empathy will come encouragement. Empathy is "our ability to 'feel into' someone else"[4]— "connecting with the emotion that someone is experiencing, not the event or the circumstance."[5] Further, as Brené Brown explains, there is no script to empathy: It's "simply listening, holding space, withholding judgment, emotionally connecting, and communicating that incredibly healing message of 'You're not alone.'"[6]

In our culture today, we struggle with each and every one of these elements. And I have become convinced this is because we are with each other less and less—we are increasingly isolated; we are off in our corners, with our people, ready for a battle at the ring of the bell. We disregard each other's humanity and forget that everyone has a story—and largely, a story of pain. Fear, anxiety, shame, and our own brokenness lead us to withdraw from others when what we need for these things to dissipate is connection.[7]

When we remain consumed by our own stuff, though, we lose track of the reality that everyone is struggling with something and that those around us are desperate to hear that they're not alone—that someone sees them and cares for them.

Years ago when I was on a very small plane with six total seats, we were bouncing around all over the place— and yet I was about as calm as I'd ever been. Why? Because the person next to me was sharing about his marriage falling apart, and I had just been through something similar. So many details reminded me of pain I had experienced, and I was able, with complete authenticity, to say, "I know what you mean," "I know how you feel," and "That is so hard." By entering into this man's story and holding space for him to share his hurt, I was able to step outside of my own fear. As I became a conduit of empathy, I was open to the Holy Spirit working through me for the benefit and good of another.

For several years now, I have been growing in empathy in a very specific way. I call it "praying with pictures." The idea came to me at some point as I was scrolling mindlessly through Facebook. At the time, the Syrian refugee crisis, which continues to this day, was just beginning. As I scrolled, the horrifying pictures began to have little effect. I thought in that moment, *What if this mindless scrolling could be redeemed?* So I decided to pray for the people in the pictures. The little girl with tears running down her face, the mother with outstretched arms, the group of boys playing with a ball in a camp. I tried to put myself inside of their stories. Of course, there was no way to know all of what they must have been feeling, but how terrifying it must have been, how heart-wrenching, how debilitating. I prayed, and as the words came, so did tears. We were worlds apart, but I suddenly felt connected to these mothers and children, fathers and brothers.

After this, I started praying for political candidates—the ones whose positions and postures I struggled with. I found pictures of them when they were children and considered what their childhoods might have been like. I began to understand, to see them as human, loved and cherished. Then I moved on to enemies—to the Taliban and terrorists, rapists and child molestors—people who are hated and considered less than human. This was the hardest group, and I'm still working at this praying practice at all levels. But as I sought to connect with others through empathy, I connected with God. He was close—as if he were sitting next to me, receiving each word and groan and thought. My heart's stinginess released a bit, and a spirit of generosity and love settled on me.

The more I've prayed with pictures, the more empathy I have not just for those for whom I'm praying but for anyone I encounter, from my family to friends to colleagues to strangers. I can listen and hold space without judgment. This empathy has expanded into encouragement. Now, as I listen to friends sharing stories with me or colleagues requesting prayer, I believe it is my responsibility to minister to their needs, to be an instrument of Christ's love in their life. Sure, they may have friends who are closer to them and spiritual mentors who advise them or help carry their burdens. But as soon as I hear another's story of pain or accomplishment, hurt or success, and I place myself in their shoes, I am equipped by God's grace and the Holy Spirit to promote their welfare and encourage their heart. If I don't do it, who will?

This is most difficult when the stories others share are of them acting in ways that aren't loving or that are dismissive of others' humanity—in these times, encouragement takes courage and relationship. As Hebrews 10:24 (NIV) says, we are to "spur one another on toward love and good deeds." This is our ministry. But more often than not, we help our friends justify their behavior or lack of love either by failing to say something because we don't want a confrontation or to come off as judgmental or by supporting them in their self-justification. If we are called to be instruments of Christ's love in the lives of others, we abandon our calling when we refuse to gently confront our fellow Christians when their actions or words don't reflect obedience to God's ways. Larry Crabb writes that "passively accepting people where they are until they get around to godly living is not a biblical strategy for encouragement."[8] We must be motivated by love and understand the fear and need that likely stands behind a particular person's actions or words. When this is the case, even rebuke and exhortation can be encouraging to the spiritual journey of another. But encouragement without empathy is generally not received well. So let us be people of courageous, intentional encouragement, noticing where our empathy needs to grow and speaking words of love and truth whenever we have the opportunity.

PRACTICE GUIDE

Because encouragement is hard for me, I've had to practice it, fail at it, and practice it again. This one will be lifelong for me, I think. I even have to question my motives sometimes; in my quest to be encouraging, I want to make sure I'm spurring people on for their sake, not so I can feel better about my ability to do so. Larry Crabb says of motives, "Nothing less than Spirit-led and Bible-provoked self-examination will enable us to recognize whether our words are self-serving or prompted by the desire to minister."[9] So, along with my suggestions about ways to practice, I must also encourage you to examine your own motivations from time to time, in God's presence and with his guidance. And don't neglect to develop your empathy muscle too, because without that, encouragement ends up being shallow and not all that edifying. As you do these things, here are some specific ways to practice encouragement:

- Celebrate big life transitions for kids so they feel special and know you're proud of them. (When I shaved my legs for the first time, around age ten or eleven, my parents got me a cake! On top, it read: "A Close

Shave." I was a little embarrassed, but at the same time, I felt proud, grown-up, and like I was really seen.)

- When you see someone act with kindness in even a small way, tell them you noticed and you were inspired and touched by what they did.

- When you go to a wedding, consider it a privilege to stand with this new couple venturing into a very hard commitment and let them know you are with them and are for their marriage. Write a note to them every now and then to let them know someone is out there who knows it's hard and worth it.

- When someone shares that they're going through a hard time, write them a short card to let them know you're thinking about them.

- Send an anonymous gift card or small amount of money to someone who's struggling. This may be the little notice they needed to keep going.

- If someone you have a relationship with posts something on Facebook that strikes you as unkind or un-Christlike, reach out to them personally and offer a gentle correction: "Hey, friend. I just saw what you posted on Facebook. I know you're feeling angry, but it seemed unkind. I know that's not your heart, so I thought I'd mention it so you realize how it came across, at least to me." I know this is a scary one. It is hard to confront a friend, but we all need this, whether we want it or not. It will grow us in love. As Dietrich Bonhoeffer wrote,

> God has willed that we should seek and find His living word in the witness of a brother, in the mouth of man. Therefore, the Christian needs another Christian who speaks God's Word to him. He needs him again and again when he becomes uncertain and discouraged, for by himself he cannot help himself without belying the truth. He needs his brother man as a bearer and proclaimer of the divine word of salvation. He needs his brother solely because of Jesus Christ. The Christ in his own heart is weaker than the Christ in the word to this brother; his own heart is uncertain, his brother's is sure.[10]

REFLECTION QUESTIONS

1. Who has been the biggest encourager in your life? How would you describe their way of encouragement to a friend?

2. How are you doing these days at developing and showing empathy? Where do you see a need for growth? Are there particular views, people, or ways

of acting that you struggle to understand? How might you take a first step into empathy?

3. Do you struggle with encouraging others? Why do you think that is? If not, who did you learn from?

4. What's the best way you have found to spur on others toward more love?

CHAPTER 8

EAT TOGETHER

Food is the daily sacrament of unnecessary goodness,
ordained for a continual remembrance that the world will
always be more delicious than it is useful. Necessity is the
mother only of clichés. It takes playfulness to make poetry.

ROBERT FARRAR CAPON

I have spent most of my life seeing the process of eating as either a necessity for the body or as a place of excess, with very little nuance in between. And I know I'm not alone in that. We are surrounded by a culture that categorizes food as good or bad, and our food choices as a direct statement on our bodies being good or bad. If something tastes particularly good, it has too much fat and too many calories. And eating healthy foods, like vegetables or legumes, requires strict discipline or lots of butter, which equals lots of fat and cholesterol. Fruits are healthy but leave us hungry. Bread has too many carbs. A heavy meal may result in our berating ourselves the next day, but eating a low-fat diet may result in little nutrition and a stomachache. Fast food is an absolute no-no, yet often a necessity due to limited options or resources. Calculations of calories and fat grams can preoccupy us, and we can see what's on our plates as a series or compilation of numbers, an approach that Robert Farrar Capon describes as "the work of the devil."[1] "The modern diet victim," he says, "sees his life at the table not as a delightful alternation between pearls of great price and dishes of lesser cost, but as a grim sentence which condemns him to pay for every fattening repast (even the sleaziest) with a meal of carrot sticks and celery."[2]

How true. I have felt all of these warring ideas—and the accompanying shame. I have pretended for years that there has been no cost, emotional or otherwise, to my feelings about food. Even now as I write, I sense the weight of shame about food weighing on me as I mentally count the calories I had yesterday and lament the fact that I didn't go for a walk to help offset what I ate. As I age and my body changes, this body/eating shame has continued to be difficult to fend off.

Yet there is hope.

In recent years, I have sensed a slow and subtle shift toward embracing food as a gift to be enjoyed and savored. The shift began when I reflected back on a dinner I had with a friend at an Ethiopian restaurant in the Chicago area. I had never been to such a restaurant and had no idea what I was in for, but I was up for trying something new. I didn't know it would be one of the most memorable experiences of my life, one that would begin to reshape the way I thought about eating. We sat at a square wooden table in the middle of the restaurant that was already set with napkins and two glasses of water without ice. The menu was incomprehensible to me, both in terms of words and pictures. I didn't know the language, and nothing captured in the photos looked familiar. I let my friend, who had been there once before, order for us and made sure to mention I'm not a fan of spicy. We talked surface-level stuff as we waited. We hadn't seen each other in years, and the conversation felt clunky and awkward—lots of uncomfortable pauses, in which I wondered what we'd ever had in common. Just when I thought I might have to run to the restroom to buy some time, the server set a large platter between us. It took up nearly the entire table, leaving just a sliver of wood where a plate might go. The platter looked like a painter's palette; it was filled with colors and textures I had never seen in my cuisine—everything from spicy meat stews (called wot) to sautéed vegetables to slaw to sauces sat atop a brownish spongy-looking substance. For a few moments I just stared at this beautiful creation. To dig into this plate felt like an act of desecration.

We had no personal plates and no silverware, but using the spongy, pancake-looking bread along the side of the platter—injera flatbread (made from the very rare teff grain)—I scooped up my first bite. The flavors and textures were varied and delicious.

But the specific taste of the food wasn't the revolutionary part of this experience. It was the dipping and sharing and conversation about the spices, sauces, and colors. We spun the platter around saying, "Try this one! It's so interesting." "Ooh, you gotta taste this one." We pulled the injera bread apart and dipped and scooped. I remember that we were smiling those wide kinds of smiles that run deeper than just our faces. Joy was radiating from us as we laughed and talked first about the food itself, enjoying the fact that we didn't know what anything was, and then about old memories and times we'd shared together years earlier. The chilies in the food started to get to us, and we downed more and more glasses of water. We laughed so hard at one point, I cried and coughed all at once. This round platter between us, made up of diverse tastes, foreign (to me) spices, and beautiful, bright colors had opened up something. Our conversation came easy, and the friendship we'd had for so long deepened and expanded. The injera was running low, and we split the last bit, tearing it across the table and laughing. Maybe it was the company, the beauty, or the common plate, but I didn't think about the calories or fat even once.

As I think about my time at the Ethiopian restaurant, it's impossible for me not to recall the story the apostle John tells near the end of his Gospel. Jesus had been crucified, and despair had settled in on those who knew him well. Several of the disciples, including Peter, resumed their prior professions and went out fishing. After a long, fishless night, they looked up and saw a man standing on the beach. The man told them to cast their nets on the right side of the boat, and to their surprise, fish filled the net to the point that they couldn't pull it in. Of course, they immediately realized the man was Jesus, and Peter couldn't help himself: He ditched the boat, dove into the sea, and swam to shore, leaving his friends to figure out how to drag in the overloaded net. When they all arrived on the beach, "they saw a fire laid, with fish and bread cooking on it" (John 21:9, MSG); "Jesus then took the bread and gave it to them. He did the same with the fish" (John 21:13, MSG). This story often forms the beginning of what scholars call "the reinstatement of Peter." And it is important for that reason. But that's not why I find it so compelling.

Whenever I read this story, I can't help but imagine that when Jesus passed around the fish or the bread, his hands touched his disciples' hands. Perhaps a bed of grass or straw or something in the center of their circle acted as a common plate, holding more fish and bread. And when they each reached for a piece, their hands touched and they fed themselves, hungry from a long night's work. They weren't worried about the germs or the grime on their hands. They weren't thinking about the ways carbs broke down into fat or the pounds the bread might add to their waistlines. They were so grateful to be eating a meal fresh from the sea with their best friends and their Lord. I imagine they were a bit apprehensive at first, given what had happened the last time they saw Jesus; before them sat a man who had been raised from the dead. But as they ate and passed the food, they loosened up, began to smile, and laughed. And eventually, their joy at the truth that Jesus had conquered their biggest fear—death—had to have spilled out.

Eating is so different now, at least in the Western world. Eating has become shrouded in shame and anxiety. We end up seeing "our bodies as a problem to be monitored rather than a gift. Instead of seeing our limits as enabling meaning and pleasure, we see our bodily limits as burdens to be superseded."[3] Again, we rebel against our humanness and refuse our limits.

We have also become accustomed to eating in a hurry and alone. The *Washington Post* called eating alone "the most American thing there is."[4] When I visited Sicily many years ago, my group of colleagues wouldn't start dinners until after 8:00 p.m. (nearing bedtime for me, these days), and then we'd spend hours upon hours at the table, eating one course after another while we talked and laughed. There was no such thing as even a quick espresso or a cup of coffee without someone else at your side. Eating took time and was communal. But I was still in my very American eating mode, glancing at my watch, thinking I had to get up early the next morning, forgetting that this eating was a gift. I was still counting calories, regretting all the carbs, and speaking not-so-nice words to myself after my third night of gelato.

Almost thirty years later, it has become increasingly common for Americans to eat alone. We eat alone in our cars, in hotel rooms, and at our desks. I knew someone who was so desperate for alone time that she went in the bathroom stall at work to eat. But by making eating such an independent enterprise, we miss out on the transformative, healing practice of eating together.

While I have a long way to go when it comes to my shame and anxiety around food, I have finally realized that eating can be spiritually significant.[5] Indeed, as L. Shannon Jung notes, "Food practices are one of God's ways of encouraging life, of resisting sin and evil, and of building community."[6] Eating alone isn't a bad thing in and of itself—but few would argue against the beauty that can happen when we eat with others. We end up better off when we eat with others: We often find ourselves built up and filled, emotionally and spiritually. This is especially true as we walk through brokenness, shame, anxiety, and fear. There is nothing quite like the intimacy of a table when you're hurting. The food provides a kind of buffer or maybe even an entry point to talk about things that matter. We can share more of ourselves as we are occupied with nourishing our bodies. Our hands and mouths are busy, and this somehow allows a space to share what's really going on. So many of the stories we read in the Gospels involve the intimacy of the table. There, we are slowed down, face-to-face, and doing one of the most fundamental actions of a created being—eating.

But how does this practice work as an offering of our whole selves—our bodies—to God? How does sharing a meal open us to an encounter with God? Why would we want to invite others to the table when we're suffering with shame, anxiety, or fear? Merely having others sitting with you at a table doesn't automatically work spiritual magic. But as we look at the practice of eating together, I'm not referring to just having additional bodies sitting around with a table between them.

Jesus accepted the invitation of a tax collector for dinner; he ate with Pharisees, who opposed him; he served food to hungry masses who'd come to listen to his words and be near to him; he ate with friends Mary, Martha, and Lazarus; he invited himself to eat with the infamous sinner Zacchaeus; he ate with Judas; and he made breakfast for the friends who, at his most agonizing moment, turned their backs on him.

Imagine yourself having meals with those with whom Jesus ate. I don't mean the actual historical people but the kinds of people—opposers, enemies, renowned sinners, the truly hungry and needy, the busy and preoccupied, the friends who dropped you when things got hard, the person who wrongly accused you and turned you in. This is not easy! Sharing a meal with those you might otherwise never have contact with because you lack a perceived commonality is a sacrifice. And eating with enemies, betrayers, or those with very different views requires courage and vulnerability. This kind of eating together necessitates turning from your own need to be built up and filled up to making an offering for the good of others and for the sake of Christ.

Eating together can be difficult. It certainly was in the early church. Food and eating laws had dominated the Jewish faith for centuries. With the gospel, though, came a new way. Now, Jews could eat with Gentiles. Nothing was considered unclean (Romans 14:14). But the squabbles and arguments about eating together sparked many words from Paul about how the "weak in faith" and the "strong in faith" were to engage one another (Romans 14); this is undoubtedly why Paul instructed the Romans to "honor one another above yourselves. . . . Share with the Lord's people who are in need. Practice hospitality" (Romans 12:10, 13, NIV).

We read "practice hospitality" today and think more narrowly than what Paul meant. He had strangers, outsiders, and nonbelievers in mind here, not friends and family.[7] Eating together would have been a sacrifice, for Jews and Gentiles—a challenge to the Jews because so much of their identity was tied to food, and a challenge to Gentiles because they relished their freedom to eat whatever they wanted. It also would have been a sacrifice for the wealthy and those held in high regard because now, with the gospel, slaves and the lowly were also welcomed and invited to the table. And consider a slave, perhaps poorly treated, willingly sharing space with his master. A sacrifice. And, in fact, a single woman might be present without her husband![8]

As a spiritual practice, eating together is a sacrifice, especially for self-centered types (which, by the way, applies to all of us). We would rather eat with people who share our views, experiences, political party, and status. It's easier. But we will only experience true community and fellowship—that is, an encounter with Christ in others[9]—when we are "overwhelmed by a great disillusionment with others, with Christians in general."[10] Eating together *as a spiritual practice* pulls us up and out of ourselves, rendering our calorie counting irrelevant. If we are suffering with shame and feeling a lack of worth, the table reminds us that we are all in need of God's grace and salvation, that we are all on equal footing:

> The table is the great equalizer, the level playing field many of us have been looking everywhere for. The table is the place where the doing stops, the trying stops, the masks are removed, and we allow ourselves to be nourished, like children. We allow someone else to meet our need. In a world that prides people on not having needs, on going longer and faster, on going without, on powering through, the table is a place of safety and rest and humanity, where we are allowed to be as fragile as we feel.[11]

In 2012, my daughter and I began the spiritual practice of eating together, hosting a dinner we called "Celebrating God's Goodness." The idea was that we would gather a group of people of all walks of life, experiences, and backgrounds in order to reflect on God's goodness to each of us over the past year. We would eat together, and share Communion, and then we would each share where we experienced God's presence and goodness. I wanted us all to see how God was at work all over the world.

I invited each person to bring a dish or some contribution to the meal and believed that intimacy would result. I also concluded that we should all sit at long tables, even if we were crammed together and the aesthetic wouldn't win me a hospitality prize. Sharing Communion was critical simply because Jesus said that when we gather, we should reenact what he did at the Last Supper in order to remember him. I wanted Jesus to be at the center of our time together.

I was sweaty-hands nervous as people began to arrive, and I thought about throwing all my ideas out and just ditching any of the sharing. I worried we'd run out of food and that my guests would end up feeling awkward because they were strangers to one another. I wondered if my American friends would say something insensitive to my African friends; or if my affluent friends might accidentally exclude my friend who was a homeless veteran; or if the law-abiding among us would judge the two friends who'd just gotten out of prison days before; or if my Democrat friends and Republican friends would spar to the point of discomfort and offense. So much could go wrong.

Instead, the unforgettable happened. Twenty-five bodies, each carrying a different burden and concern, arrived. Christ was in and among us. As the people around the table stabbed at the beef brisket, lifted pasta and green salads to their tongues, buttered their rolls, and sipped their wine or water, they dropped their defenses, fears, and judgments. We could touch the vulnerability in the air, and each of us held it gently so we could share in it together. As the moments passed and each person spoke, we all wondered (I found this out later) whether we had ever experienced before or would ever experience again what we experienced that night around the table.

The conversation didn't stay in the shallow end of the pool. We dove deep—going to places like, "I am going through a divorce and my heart is broken, but I see God here and I see God there." We didn't spend time discussing so-and-so's front-row parking spot at a crowded concert venue. We delved into the pain of mental illness and celebrated the small victories of medicine and other treatment. We spoke of gaining friends, recovering from addiction, getting freed from prison, spending seven nights and not just two in a safe shelter, using every dime to set up feeding programs for hungry orphans. Our hearts were cracked open together, and love and hope filled us. Some might read this and sigh from its heaviness. And yes, it was heavy, but it was altogether human—vulnerable, dependent, hopeful, limited. This is the result of the spiritual practice of eating together.

I held this dinner for six years straight, and each year seemed to top the one before in terms of intimacy and vulnerability. Different folks joined in, and others couldn't make it. I feared that without the same group, the dynamics would change and we'd lose out (as if *I* had created what happened or had any control over what would occur). But every time, Christ was present with us as our hands touched our lips and we partook of the food we had each made.

But I have to be honest: These meals were a sacrifice for me and my daughter. Renting the furniture we needed was pricey. Setting aside the time to make the food was never easy. Overcoming our social anxiety (it runs in the family) took energy and courage. Putting together the invite list required thought and risk. Setting up and cleaning up was exhausting. But what I wanted more than anything was for those who walked through my door to feel honored, loved, and accepted. I wanted them to remember the love of Christ as they reflected on their own stories and experiences of that year. And for those few hours we gathered together, I felt outside myself—able to rest in the present, neither regretting the past nor worrying about the future. Just present and alive. Grateful and content. Some of my most poignant memories have come from "Celebrating God's Goodness" dinners.

What happens when we meet together like this, over food, serving our bodies with what they need to laugh and cry? Social support. Community. Healing. Wholeness. Those who attended these dinners at my house looked forward to them each year and longed for the space to be seen and heard. Keep in mind that many of these people had seen counselors and had audiences who would listen to them with great attention. This was different because of the reciprocity among those who attended. We all felt heard and seen, but we also listened to and looked at one another. We were all in this thing called life together, and no one was alone in what they were experiencing.

Studies have shown that when we "are held in someone else's mind and heart," we are less likely to be overwhelmed by stress and trauma.[12] More importantly, though, when we eat together and call our table the place where we recognize Jesus in one another, we, as writer and speaker Preston Yancey writes, "radically affirm the words of Jesus when he says, 'For where two or three are gathered in my name, there am I among them.'"[13] And when we eat together as a practice for one another, we bear one another's burdens (Galatians 6:2). I love how Daniel Taylor puts it:

> As a member of a fellowship of believers, I do not have to hold together the whole complex of Christian faith and practice by myself. I do not have to do everything that the whole body of Christ should do or be everything it should be. In a sense, I do not even have to believe without ever faltering everything the body of Christ should believe.[14]

When we practice eating together, we believe for one another, bear each other's burdens—and bear with one another in love (Ephesians 4:2). And what do we need more when consumed with our brokenness, shame, anxiety, and fear? We need someone to carry these with us, to hear and see our pain, and to have faith where ours is faltering. Can we do this over coffee or on a park bench? Yes and no. I'm not sure I will ever understand the healing powers of eating together. But my guess is that it has to do with what we're saying when we come together and eat. Without meaning it, we are saying we have needs that we cannot meet—that we are not God but human. We have physical needs that can only be met with food, and we have emotional needs that can only be met by others, and we have spiritual needs that can only be met by Christ among us.

PRACTICE GUIDE

Practicing eating together, as with any other spiritual practice, requires intentionality. The sacrificial nature of such events makes them impossible to just fall into—especially in our culture today, when societal inertia pulls us toward either eating alone or with those with whom we agree and look like. You don't need to invite twenty-five people or even five. Sharing a meal with just two people is plenty. And although there is no question that intimacy and spiritual depth can happen over food with close friends and family (don't forgo such meals), this spiritual practice requires a level of sacrifice that isn't typically present in our own circles. That said, with a little more intentionality, we can transform our ordinary meals with close friends and family and create an environment of intimacy. In either context, though, intentionality is key to create an environment of intimacy that goes beyond weather and sports. You can go into a meal with a few questions in mind to take the conversation to a deeper level.

Here are some ideas on how to host a meal:

- Make the meal from scratch instead of going out or ordering in.
- Set the table a little more formally than normal to make your guests feel honored.
- Spend time praying for and thinking about your guest list.
- Consider what small touch would make each individual feel personally seen.
- Bake bread.
- Invite each guest to bring something (doesn't have to be homemade).
- Prepare intentional questions that you can insert into the conversation. Sometimes it feels awkward, but it can lead to amazing conversations and connections. Here are a few questions I've enjoyed:
  - How's your heart these days?
  - Is there anything weighing on you? What's making you particularly happy right now?
  - What do you think God's working on in you?

REFLECTION QUESTIONS

1. What about eating together sparks anxiety, shame, or fear?

2. What is your relationship with food like? If it has changed over time, how so?

3. Reflect on your most memorable meal. What made it so memorable?

4. Who do you most look forward to sharing a meal with? Why?

5. If you were to host a dinner that would be a sacrifice, who would you invite? What would you prepare?

EPILOGUE

We find ourselves so very weary, don't we, holding together all these broken parts of our souls? Roiling with anxiety and fear, holding off shame, and struggling against brokenness take away from the life Jesus came to give us. We're often exhausted because most of us have sought to deal with these parts of ourselves in ways the world teaches. We distract, numb, and escape. We hide, disconnect, and withdraw. But Jesus offers us a different way—he invites us to come to him, to drink the water he offers, and to eat the bread of life. And the apostle Paul—and indeed, the whole of Scripture—shows us how: to offer ourselves to God, body, mind, and soul, by accepting our humanness and turning away from the patterns of the world by giving ourselves over in the service to and uplifting of others.

None of this comes naturally. Turning toward life-giving holy vulnerability takes practice, practice, practice.

Practice seeing where we have withdrawn ourselves from God and his ways and are experiencing unholy leakage. Practice recognizing our coping practices—all the ways we seek to run from or cover up our broken pieces, shame, anxiety, and fear.

But oh! What awaits us on the other side as we practice being in God's presence. Come, my friend, and receive Jesus' invitation to rest. Surrender in the midst of your vulnerability, lean on the faith and hope of others through common prayer, laugh out loud and find life in joy, ground yourself in the earth God has provided, encourage those around you, and meet Christ at the table through meaningful interactions with those he loves.

As we allow God to meet us in our humanity, through our humanity, the negative emotions and temptations that pull at us will dissipate. We will find ourselves transformed, day by day, not wholly healed but moving toward healing. In the restoration of God's presence, holy vulnerability will sing through the cracks and shattered pieces and wounds of our lives, and we will see that the very areas of broken humanity that have plagued us for so long are what have drawn us closer to him. We will realize that we are increasingly able to love God and others sacrificially, selflessly, and wholly, to offer what we have been given, and to rest in the presence of the one who loves us.

May it be so!

Acknowledgments

To my God—Father, Son, and Spirit—thank you for saving me in the midst of my brokenness. Thank you for transforming, healing, opening, and loving me, even as I struggle to trust you. I offer my whole self to you and pray I would, by my life, demonstrate your love and care for the broken, ashamed, anxious, and afraid.

To my friends and colleagues that were part of the MANT '16 cohort at Northern Seminary: So much of what is in this book indwells me because of our time together in class, at lunch, in Paul's actual footsteps, and on my back deck (possibly in the hot tub). I am especially thankful to you, Scot McKnight, for seeing something in me that I didn't see and inviting me to go to seminary. Thank you for your encouragement, counsel, and friendship.

To the Willow Creek Community Church congregation and staff: Thank you for trusting me enough to invite me into your brokenness, shame, anxiety, and fear. I am so grateful and honored to have so many opportunities to hold space for you and be present with you when things are hard or confusing. It has been in your vulnerability that I have seen God at work and have been inspired to expose my own vulnerability as a way to find wholeness and healing.

To Don Pape: Thank you for believing in me and encouraging me. You have been a gift.

To Caitlyn Carlson: Thank you for walking with me through every step of this book. Thanks for listening to my struggles, encouraging me when I didn't think I could write another word, believing for me that I would get this book done, and making the book better. Thanks most of all for seeing me.

To my soul friends, Michael Fox, Amy Radeck, Joy DeLaere, Aaron Niequist, John and Jenna Perrine, Stella Kasirye, Martha Temfwe, Lori Shoults, Sandra McFarland, and Rhianna Godfrey: Thank you for showing me Jesus.

To Cameron and Laniyla: Thank you for bringing life, laughter, and fun to our lives. I can't imagine not knowing and loving you. You're both smart, funny, and sweet. Always. Breanna, thanks for being brave and trusting us with your beautiful, amazing kids.

To Mom: Thank you for modeling what it looks like to sacrifice and love with joy, patience, and endurance. To Dorsey: I miss you. Wish you were here so I could show you this book. Turns out what I remember most is your silly smile, our games of Monopoly, and you believing in me, no matter the endeavor. To Dad: Thank you for modeling a life of curiosity about how the world works and for your steadfastness. To Anna: Thank you for showing me what a life of hospitality looks like, and for teaching me the importance of good cooking and gardening. To Tracey: Thank you for inspiring me with your generosity of spirit and desire for adventure. To Kendall: Thank you for gifting our family with your creativity and care and, of course, for bringing Tyler and Barnaby into our lives. To Lucy: Thank you for modeling a deep love for animals, music, and family. I can't wait to see all you'll continue to bring into the world.

To Fern: Thank you for teaching me how to trim the rose bushes and for allowing me the absolute privilege of helping to care for you and listen to your childhood stories in your last years.

To Jaclyn: You have more energy and excitement for living than anyone I know. You bring goodness and joy into every room. Thank you for being a source of light and kindness to me.

To Kalyn: You have a tender heart and a sensitive soul. Thank you for being present where you are and listening so well.

To Jamie: My sweets, you are a gentle, kind, creative, intentional, loving soul. Thank you for all that you've taught me as you've grown up, the cherished friend you have become, and the greatest demonstration of God's love to me.

To Steve: Thank you for loving me in all my brokenness, shame, anxiety, and fear. You have seen all of me and have loved me more and more. I didn't know this was possible. God has shown me his love through you. Thank you for encouraging me in my writing and your ever-willingness to listen to a sentence or turn of phrase from some random book I'm reading.

INTRODUCTION

1. Daniel Taylor, *The Myth of Certainty: The Reflective Christian and the Risk of Commitment* (Downers Grove, IL: InterVarsity Press, 1992), 22.
2. Richard Rohr, *Breathing Under Water: Spirituality and the Twelve Steps* (Cincinnati: Franciscan Media, 2011), xxi.
3. This idea comes from Parker J. Palmer's *On the Brink of Everything: Grace, Gravity, and Getting Old* (Oakland, CA: Berrett-Koehler, 2018), 57. He says that "contemplation is any way one has of penetrating illusion and touching reality."

PART I: NOTICING OUR ABSENCE

1. Ida Korneliussen, "Why Do We Dread the Dentist?" ScienceNormay.no, February 6, 2013, https://sciencenorway.no/fear-of-dentists-forskningno -norway/why-do-we-dread-the-dentist/1382301.

CHAPTER 1: NOTICING OUR NEED

1. Richard Rohr, *Breathing Under Water: Spirituality and the Twelve Steps* (Cincinnati: Franciscan Media, 2011), 3.
2. Ronald Rolheiser, *Sacred Fire: A Vision for a Deeper Human and Christian Maturity* (New York: Image, 2014), 83.
3. This is not the little girl's real name.
4. Cornelius Plantinga Jr., *Not the Way It's Supposed to Be: A Breviary of Sin* (Grand Rapids, MI: Eerdmans, 1996), x.
5. Ibid., 14.
6. Ibid., 10.
7. C. S. Lewis, *Mere Christianity* (New York: HarperCollins, 2001), 101.
8. Brené Brown's teaching is insightful, research-based, and easy to follow. If shame is something you really struggle with, I recommend reading

and listening to Brené Brown. You might start with one (or more!) of these resources: Brené Brown, *The Power of Vulnerability: Teachings on Vulnerability, Connection, and Courage,* read by the author, Louisville, CO: Sounds True, 2013, audio recording, 6 hr., 30 min.; Brené Brown, "Listening to Shame," TED2012, March 2012, https://www.ted.com/talks/brene_brown_listening_to_shame/transcript?language=en; and Brené Brown, "The Power of Vulnerability," TEDxHouston, June 2010, https://www.ted.com/talks/brene_brown_the_power_of_vulnerability?language=en.

9. Brené Brown, *Daring Greatly: How the Courage to Be Vulnerable Transforms the Way We Live, Love, Parent, and Lead* (New York: Avery, 2015), 69.
10. Ibid., 69.
11. Bruce K. Waltke, *Genesis: A Commentary* (Grand Rapids, MI: Zondervan, 2001), 92.
12. Brown, *Daring Greatly*, chap. 3.
13. Ibid., 99.
14. Edmund Bourne and Lorna Garano, *Coping with Anxiety: Ten Simple Ways to Relieve Anxiety, Fear & Worry* (Oakland, CA: New Harbinger, 2016), 8.
15. Ibid., 3.
16. Ibid., 2.
17. Brown, *Daring Greatly*, 140.
18. As quoted in James Porter Moreland, *Finding Quiet: My Story of Overcoming Anxiety and the Practices that Brought Peace* (Grand Rapids, MI: Zondervan, 2019), 76.
19. There is something of a debate as to whether Scripture actually includes 365 instances in which God tells his people not to fear (see, for example, https://aleteia.org/2017/08/27/if-you-suffer-from-anxiety-you-need-to-know-the-most-repeated-advice-in-the-bible/ and https://www.accordancebible.com/A-Do-Not-Be-Afraid-For-Every-Day-Of-The-Year). But whether this assertion is accurate is not really my point. As I explain, willing ourselves to be fearless doesn't seem to be what God is meaning to say. Rather, his instructions about fear are more of an invitation to be aware of his presence and faithfulness to us in the midst of situations that elicit fear.
20. Drawn from "Dr. Albrecht's 5 Types of Fears: What We're Really Afraid Of," Coaching Tools, October 2, 2014, https://www.thecoachingtoolscompany.com/5-types-of-fears-dr-karl-albrecht/.
21. Italics in this list were added.

CHAPTER 2: RECOGNIZING OUR COPING PRACTICES

1. "Moravian Moment #22—The Influence of the Transformed Life," Moravian Church, Eastern West Indies Province, accessed August 12, 2020, http://moravians.net/joomla/about-us/34-moravian-moments/92 -moravian-moment-22.

2. John Wesley eventually experienced a true conversion upon the influence of the Moravian leader Peter Boehler. John D. Woodbridge and Frank A. James III, *Church History, Volume Two: From Pre-Reformation to the Present Day* (Grand Rapids, MI: Zondervan, 2013), 407.

3. Rowan Williams, *Being Human: Bodies, Minds, Persons* (Grand Rapids, MI: Eerdmans, 2018), 43.

4. Cornelius Plantinga Jr., *Not the Way It's Supposed to Be: A Breviary of Sin* (Grand Rapids, MI: Eerdmans, 1996), 125.

5. Mark Sayers, *Strange Days: Life in the Spirit in a Time of Upheaval* (Chicago: Moody, 2017), 34.

6. Parker J. Palmer, *On the Brink of Everything: Grace, Gravity, and Getting Old* (Oakland, CA: Berrett-Koehler, 2018), 152.

7. David Whyte, "David Whyte: The Conversational Nature of Reality," interview by Krista Tippett, *On Being*, April 7, 2016, https://onbeing .org/programs/david-whyte-the-conversational-nature-of-reality/.

8. Richard Rohr, *Breathing Under Water: Spirituality and the Twelve Steps* (Cincinnati: Franciscan Media, 2011), 18.

9. Joseph Burgo, *Why Do I Do That?: Psychological Defense Mechanisms and the Hidden Ways They Shape Our Lives* (Chapel Hill, NC: New Rise Press, 2012), 6, 10.

10. Ibid., 50, 55, 65, 68, 86, 99, 115, 130–131.

11. Ibid., 69.

12. Ibid., 182.

13. Ibid., 182.

14. Brené Brown, *Daring Greatly: How the Courage to Be Vulnerable Transforms the Way We Live, Love, Parent, and Lead* (New York: Avery, 2015), 138.

15. "Your habitual ways of interacting with the important people in your life tell us a great deal about the defense mechanisms you typically use" (Burgo, *Why Do I Do That?*, 12).

16. Brown, *Daring Greatly*, 147.

PART II: PRACTICING GOD'S PRESENCE

1. Richard N. Longenecker, *The Epistle to the Romans*, New International Greek Testament Commentary (Grand Rapids, MI: Eerdmans, 2016), 920.

2. N. T. Wright, "Romans Commentary" in *The New Interpreter's Bible Commentary*, vol. IX (Nashville: Abingdon Press, 2015), 606.

3. Scot McKnight, *Reading Romans Backwards: A Gospel of Peace in the Midst of Empire* (Waco: Baylor University Press, 2019), 30.

4. Ibid., 30–31.

5. Ibid., 36.

6. Ibid., 36.

7. See Romans 7:22-25.

CHAPTER 3: SURRENDER YOUR BODY

1. See Dallas Willard, *The Spirit of the Disciplines: Understanding How God Changes Lives* (New York: HarperOne, 1991), 37.

2. See Jane E. Vennard, *Praying with Body and Soul: A Way to Intimacy with God* (Minneapolis: Augsburg Fortress, 1998), 19, which describes the ways the body has been treated throughout Christian history.

3. David G. Benner, *Surrender to Love: Discovering the Heart of Christian Spirituality* (Downers Grove, IL: InterVarsity Press, 2015), 61.

4. Ibid., 61–62.

5. Willard, *Spirit of the Disciplines*, 30–31.

6. Benner, *Surrender*, 17.

7. Richard Rohr, *Breathing Under Water: Spirituality and the Twelve Steps* (Cincinnati: Franciscan Media, 2011), 18.

8. C. S. Lewis, *Mere Christianity* (New York: HarperCollins, 1952), 197.

9. Willard, *Spirit of the Disciplines*, xi.

10. Richard Rohr, *What the Mystics Know: Seven Pathways to Your Deeper Self* (New York: Crossroad, 2015), 78.

11. Rowan Williams, *Being Human: Bodies, Minds, Persons* (Grand Rapids, MI: Eerdmans, 2018), 63; "Our human mental processes, and spiritual processes, are perpetually seduced by the model of *escape* and the model of *control*."

CHAPTER 4: PRAY COMMON PRAYERS

1. Jane E. Vennard, *Praying with Body and Soul: A Way to Intimacy with God* (Minneapolis: Augsburg Fortress, 1998), 46.

2. See Scot McKnight, *Praying with the Church: Following Jesus Daily, Hourly, Today* (Brewster, MA; Paraclete Press, 2006), 3–4.

3. Ibid., 3.

4. Ibid., ix.

5. Ibid., 45–46.

6. Phyllis Tickle, *The Divine Hours: Prayers for Autumn and Wintertime* (New York: Doubleday, 2000), x.

7. Ibid., xi.

8. The daily offices include: Matins (nighttime), Lauds (early morning), Prime (first hour of daylight), Terce (third hour), Sext (noon), None (ninth hour), Vespers (evening), and Compline (end of the day). McKnight, *Praying*, 104–105.

9. Tickle, *Divine Hours*, xi.

10. Bobby Gross, *Living the Christian Year: Time to Inhabit the Story of God* (Downers Grove, IL: IVP Books, 2009), 17.

11. Eric E. Peterson, *Letters to a Young Congregation: Nurturing the Growth of a Faithful Church* (Colorado Springs: NavPress, 2020), "Compensation Package" letter.

12. Ibid., "Compensation Package."

13. McKnight, *Praying*, 18.

14. Daniel Taylor, *The Myth of Certainty: The Reflective Christian and the Risk of Commitment* (Downers Grove, IL: InterVarsity Press, 1992), 110.

15. Shane Claiborne, *Common Prayer: A Liturgy for Ordinary Radicals* (Grand Rapids, MI: Zondervan, 2010), 12.

16. *The Book of Common Prayer* (New York: The Episcopal Church, 2007), 383–84. For easy access, see https://www.bcponline.org/.

17. Ibid., 816.

18. Ted Loder, *Guerrillas of Grace: Prayers for the Battle* (Minneapolis: Augsburg Books, 2005), 40.

19. McKnight, *Praying*, 161.

20. "A Collect for Grace," from *The Book of Common Prayer*, Morning Prayer II.

21. See https://oneyearbibleonline.com/daily-oyb/.

22. "Confession of Sin," from *The Book of Common Prayer*, Evening Prayer II.

23. "A Collect for Protection," from *The Book of Common Prayer*, Evening Prayer II.

24. Adaptation of "A Collect for Aid against Perils," from *The Book of Common Prayer*, Evening Prayer II.
Citations for listed prayer books follow.
Book of Psalms, in the Bible (translation of your choice).
Shane Claiborne, *Common Prayer: A Liturgy for Ordinary Radicals* (Grand Rapids, MI: Zondervan, 2010).
Desmond Tutu, *An African Prayer Book* (New York: Doubleday, 1995).
Phyllis Tickle, *The Divine Hours: Prayers for Summertime* (New York: Doubleday, 2000).
Phyllis Tickle, *The Divine Hours: Prayers for Autumn and Wintertime* (New York: Doubleday, 2000).

Phyllis Tickle, *The Divine Hours: Prayers for Springtime* (New York: Doubleday, 2001).

Ted Loder, *Guerrillas of Grace: Prayers for the Battle* (Minneapolis: Augsburg Books, 2005).

Benedictine Daily Prayer: A Short Breviary, 2nd ed. (Collegeville, MN: Liturgical Press, 2015).

The Book of Common Prayer (New York: The Episcopal Church, 2007).

Kellye Fabian, *Sacred Questions: A Transformative Journey through the Bible* (Colorado Springs: NavPress, 2018).

25. *The Little Book of Hours: Praying with the Community of Jesus*, rev. ed. (Brewster, MA: Paraclete Press, 2007).

CHAPTER 5: LAUGH OUT LOUD

1. Jürgen Moltmann, "Christianity: A Religion of Joy," in *Joy and Human Flourishing: Essays on Theology, Culture, and the Good Life*, ed. Miroslav Volf and Justine E. Crisp (Minneapolis: Fortress Press, 2015), 14.

2. To read about the story we heard, read Tricia Lott Williford, *And Life Comes Back: A Wife's Story of Love, Loss, and Hope Reclaimed* (Colorado Springs: WaterBrook, 2014).

3. Daniel Taylor, *The Myth of Certainty: The Reflective Christian and the Risk of Commitment* (Downers Grove, IL: InterVarsity Press, 1992), 137.

4. Brian Edgar, *Laughter and the Grace of God: Restoring Laughter to Its Central Role in Christian Spirituality and Theology* (Eugene, OR: Cascade Books, 2019), 26.

5. James Martin, *Between Heaven and Mirth: Why Joy, Humor, and Laughter Are at the Heart of the Spiritual Life* (New York: HarperOne, 2012), 20.

6. Edgar, *Laughter*, 19.

7. Ibid., 14.

8. For a fuller explanation of laughter in the Bible, see Brian Edgar, *Laughter and the Grace of God*; and James Martin, *Between Heaven and Mirth*, 20.

9. Edgar, *Laughter*, chap. 3.

10. Ibid., chap. 3.

11. Brian King, *The Laughing Cure: Emotional and Physical Healing—A Comedian Reveals Why Laughter Really Is the Best Medicine* (New York: Skyhorse, 2016), "Speaking of Laughter . . ." chap.

12. Ibid., introduction.

13. Ibid., introduction.

14. Ibid., introduction.

15. Edgar, *Laughter*, 99.

16. Julian of Norwich, "A Revelation of Love," in *The Broadview Anthology of British Literature: Volume 1, The Medieval Period*, 3rd ed. (Peterborough, Ontario: Broadview Press, 2015), 624.
17. King, *Laughing Cure*, "Practice Laughter, and Laugh Often" chap.
18. Barbara A. Holmes, *Joy Unspeakable: Contemplative Practice of the Black Church* (Minneapolis: Fortress Press, 2004), 76.
19. Ibid., 76.
20. Ibid., 77.

CHAPTER 6: DIG IN THE DIRT

1. "Lexicon: Strong's H6944—*qodesh*," Blue Letter Bible, accessed October 8, 2020, https://www.blueletterbible.org/lang/lexicon/lexicon .cfm?Strongs=H6944&t=NIV.
2. Ronald Rolheiser, *Wrestling with God: Finding Hope and Meaning in Our Daily Struggles to Be Human* (New York: Image, 2019), 27.
3. Janice Elsheimer, *Garden Graces: The Wisdom in Growing Things* (Kansas City: Nazarene Publishing House, 2015), preface.

CHAPTER 7: ENCOURAGE OTHERS

1. Larry Crabb with Dan Allender, *Encouragement: The Unexpected Power of Building Others Up* (Grand Rapids, MI: Zondervan, 2013), chap. 5.
2. Ibid., chap. 6.
3. Ibid., chap. 4.
4. Bessel van der Kolk, *The Body Keeps the Score: Brain, Mind, and Body in the Healing of Trauma* (New York: Penguin, 2014), 58.
5. Brené Brown, *Daring Greatly: How the Courage to Be Vulnerable Transforms the Way We Live, Love, Parent, and Lead* (New York: Avery, 2015), 81.
6. Ibid., 81.
7. Ibid., 74–75.
8. Crabb and Allender, *Encouragement*, chap. 8.
9. Crabb and Allender, *Encouragement*, chap. 5.
10. Dietrich Bonhoeffer, *Life Together: The Classic Exploration of Faith in Community* (New York: HarperOne, 1993), 23.

CHAPTER 8: EAT TOGETHER

1. Robert Farrar Capon, *The Supper of the Lamb: A Culinary Reflection* (Garden City, NY: Doubleday, 1969), 25.
2. Ibid., 25–26.
3. L. Shannon Jung, *Sharing Food: Christian Practices for Enjoyment* (Minneapolis: Fortress Press, 2006), 102.

4. Roberto A. Ferdman, "The Most American Thing There Is: Eating Alone," *Washington Post*, August 18, 2015, https://www.washingtonpost .com/news/wonk/wp/2015/08/18/eating-alone-is-a-fact-of-modern -american-life/.

5. Jung, *Sharing Food*, chap. 1.

6. Ibid., 19.

7. James D. G. Dunn, *The Theology of Paul the Apostle* (Grand Rapids, MI: Eerdmans, 1998), 677–79.

8. Scot McKnight illuminates the chaotic, boundary-breaking scene that would have been the church in his book *Fellowship of Differents*. Scot McKnight, *Fellowship of Differents: Showing the World God's Design for Life Together* (Grand Rapids, MI: Zondervan, 2015), 96–97.

9. "For around the table Jesus meets us, for around the table we meet Jesus in each other." Preston Yancey, *Out of the House of Bread: Satisfying Your Hunger for God with the Spiritual Disciplines* (Grand Rapids, MI: Zondervan, 2016), 148.

10. Dietrich Bonhoeffer, *Life Together: The Classic Exploration of Faith in Community* (New York: HarperOne, 1993), 27.

11. Shauna Niequist, *Bread and Wine: A Love Letter to Life Around the Table, with Recipes* (Grand Rapids, MI: Zondervan, 2013), 258.

12. Bessel van der Kolk, *The Body Keeps the Score: Brain, Mind, and Body in the Healing of Trauma* (New York: Penguin, 2014), 81.

13. Yancey, *Out of the House of Bread*, 144.

14. Daniel Taylor, *The Myth of Certainty: The Reflective Christian and the Risk of Commitment* (Downers Grove, IL: InterVarsity Press, 1992), 110.